RESIDENTIAL CONSTRUCTION
Understanding the Basics

A Guide for Anyone who Needs to Understand
the Construction of a Single-Family Home

By

Nate MacIntyre

© 2024 Nate MacIntyre This book, "RESIDENTIAL CONSTRUCTION: Understanding the Basics" is written by Nate MacIntyre and is copyrighted © 2024 Nate MacIntyre. All rights are reserved. No part of this publication may be reproduced, distributed, or transmitted in any form or by any means, including photocopying, recording, or other electronic or mechanical methods, without the prior written permission from Nate MacIntyre.

This book is dedicated to:

All the incredible and wise experts that I have had the fortune of learning from throughout my career. Also, my wonderful family and friends.

This book is intended to serve as a reference guide for understanding the construction of a single-family home. The information contained within is for informational purposes only and should not be relied upon for legal purposes. The author and publisher make no representations or warranties with respect to the accuracy or completeness of the contents of this book and specifically disclaim all warranties, including without limitation warranties of fitness for a particular purpose. No warranty may be created or extended by sales representatives or written sales materials. The advice and strategies contained herein may not be suitable for your situation. You should consult with a professional where appropriate. Neither the publisher nor the author shall be liable for any loss of profit or any other commercial damages, including but not limited to special, incidental, consequential, or other damages.

Table of Contents

Introduction 1

PART I: The Forces a Residential Structure is Designed and Built to Withstand . 7

    Chapter One: Planning and Development 20

    Chapter Two: Infrastructure, Site Preparation & Grading 25

PART II: Construction 32

    Chapter Three: Trenches, Utilities, Hardware, and Footings 34

    Chapter Four: Sand Layer, Moisture Barrier, Slab Foundation, and Crawlspaces 40

    Chapter Five: General Framing 50

    Chapter Six: Mechanical, Electrical, and Plumbing (MEP) 58

    Chapter Seven: Exterior Flashing and Waterproofing 63

    Chapter Eight: Roof Assemblies 69

    Chapter Nine: Exterior Cladding and Assemblies 75

    Chapter Ten: Interior Finishes Part 1 82

    Chapter Eleven: Interior Finishes Part 2 88

    Chapter Twelve: Maintenance 93

    Chapter Thirteen: Safety 98

    Chapter Fourteen: Technology 101

    Chapter Fifteen: Legal Matters 104

    Glossary   107

About the Author 109

Introduction

"The ideal architect should be a man of letters, a skilled draftsman, a mathematician, familiar with historical studies, a diligent student of philosophy, acquainted with music, not ignorant of medicine, learned in the responses of jurisconsults, familiar with astronomy and astronomical calculations."

Vitruvius

The Symphony of Construction

The construction of a single-family home is a marvel of modern engineering and collaboration. Over 10,000 distinct components unite to create not just a structure, but a sanctuary for future inhabitants. This introduction chapter sets the stage for understanding the intricate ballet of elements and expertise that culminates in the creation of a home.

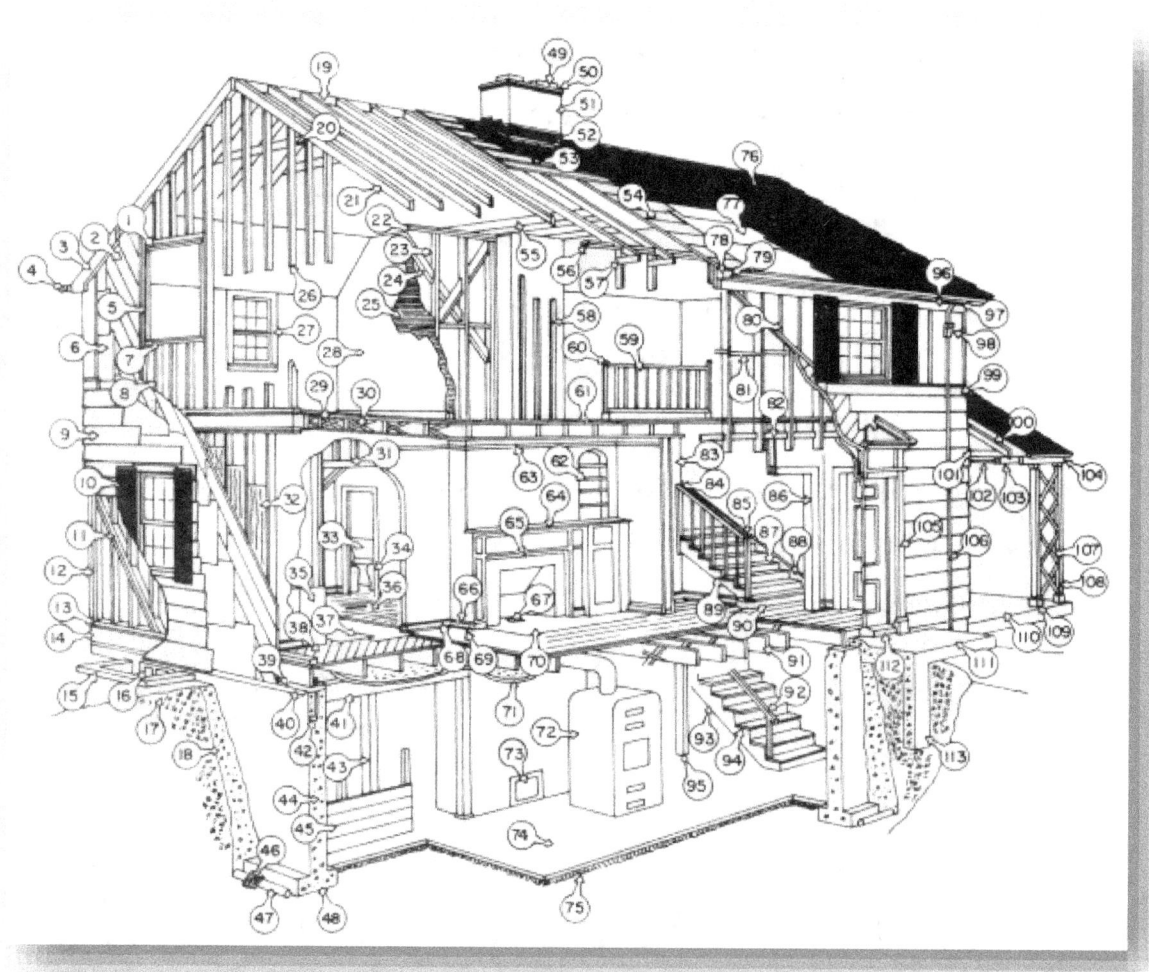

The Foundation of Stability: At the base, the foundation is laid with precision, incorporating rebar, wire ties, and mechanical anchors. Vapor barriers, rigid insulation, and fluid-applied waterproofing form a bulwark against the elements, ensuring the longevity of the structure.

Framing - The Skeleton of the Home: The framing rises from the foundation, a network of capillary breaks, sole plates, trimmers, and headers. Top plates and floor diaphragms are secured with an array of fasteners, all reinforced by hurricane hardware and steel moment frames to withstand nature's fury.

Mechanical Systems - The Breath of the House: The mechanical systems weave through the frame, a complex array of fans, termination covers, ductwork, and return plenums. Dampeners, air handlers, condensers, evaporator coils, and line sets work in concert to provide comfort and air quality.

Electrical Systems - The Nervous System: The electrical systems form the nervous system of the home, with lighting fixtures, wiring, receptacles, and switches. Circuit breakers and disconnects ensure safety and control, distributing energy to where it's needed.

Plumbing Systems - The Circulatory Network: The plumbing systems act as the circulatory network, with supply lines and drainpipes intricately running through the structure. Nail plates, mineral wool, fire caulking, and air leakage blocks are meticulously installed, ensuring functionality and safety.

Roof Assemblies - The Protective Shield: Above, roof assemblies are constructed with trusses, fascia, and underlayment. Shingles or tiles are laid with precision, while flashing, sealants, mortar, and foam provide a protective shield from the weather.

Exterior - The Home's Armor: The exterior is wrapped in a weather-resistant barrier, an air barrier, and a drainage plane. Flexible and rigid flashings, tapes, and sealants guard against moisture, while lath, mortar, finish coatings, paints, and plant-ons give the home its aesthetic appeal.

Site - The Canvas: The site itself is prepared with subgrade drainage, landscaping, and hardscaping features. Grass, trees, bushes, walkways, patios, driveways, and irrigation systems are thoughtfully designed to complement the home and its surroundings.

The Orchestra of Professionals: A diverse group of professionals orchestrates this symphony of construction. Land acquisition experts, developers, architects, drafters, engineers, municipal authorities, contracting teams, and skilled tradespeople each play a pivotal role. Their collective expertise ensures that the project is well-designed, financially sound, legally compliant, and expertly constructed.

As we delve into the subsequent chapters, we will explore each of these components and the roles of these professionals in greater detail. Their collaborative efforts result in a structure that not only meets the client's needs but also stands as a testament to human ingenuity and the enduring quest for shelter and comfort.

In the construction of a typical single-family home, a staggering array of over 10,000 distinct components come together to form a cohesive structure. These components span across various systems and assemblies:

- **Foundation**: Incorporates elements like rebar, wire ties, mechanical anchors, vapor barriers, rigid insulation, and fluid-applied waterproofing.
- **Framing**: Comprises capillary breaks, sole plates, trimmers, headers, top plates, floor diaphragms, and fasteners such as nails, screws, and glues, reinforced by hurricane hardware and steel moment frames.
- **Mechanical Systems**: Encompasses fans, termination covers, ductwork, return plenums, dampeners, air handlers, condensers, evaporator coils, and line sets.
- **Electrical Systems**: Consists of lighting fixtures, wiring, receptacles, switches, circuit breakers, and disconnects.
- **Plumbing Systems**: Includes supply lines, drain and vent pipes, nail plates, mineral wool, fire caulking, air leakage blocks, valves, and connections.
- **Roof Assemblies**: Features trusses, fascia, underlayment, shingles or tiles, flashing, sealants, mortar, and foam.
- **Exterior**: Comprises the weather-resistant barrier (WRB), air barrier, drainage plane, both flexible and rigid flashings, tapes, sealants, lath, mortar, finish coatings, paints, and plant-ons.

- **Site**: Involves subgrade drainage, landscaping elements like grass, trees, and bushes, as well as hardscaping features such as walkways, patios, driveways, and irrigation systems.

Each professional involved in the construction process plays a pivotal role in ensuring the project's success:

- **Land Acquisition and Feasibility Experts**: They assess the viability of the project site, considering zoning laws, planning requirements, and infrastructure needs. Their work lays the groundwork for a project's location and legal feasibility.
- **Developers**: They are responsible for the financial and strategic planning of the project. They work with various stakeholders to secure funding, manage investments, and oversee the project's economic viability.
- **Architects and Draftsmen**: Architects design the structure, considering aesthetics, functionality, and safety, while drafters create detailed drawings that translate the architect's vision into technical blueprints.
- **Engineers**: This group includes surveyors, geotechnical, civil, structural, mechanical, electrical, and plumbing engineers, each specializing in a critical aspect of the building's design and integrity.
- **Municipal Authorities**: Plans examiners, permit processors, building inspectors, and fire marshals ensure that the project complies with all local codes and regulations, which is essential for the safety and legality of the construction.
- **Contracting Team**: This team manages the day-to-day operations of the construction site. Estimators calculate costs, project managers oversee the project's progress, and superintendents handle on-site operations.
- **Skilled Tradespeople**: These are the individuals who physically build the structure. They include concrete workers, masons, carpenters, electricians, plumbers, ironworkers, roofers, and HVAC technicians, each bringing specialized skills to the project.

Each professional's expertise contributes to a different facet of the construction process, from conceptualization to completion, ensuring that the project is well-designed, financially sound, legally compliant, and expertly constructed. Their collaborative efforts result in a structure that meets the client's needs and stands the test of time.

This book aims to demystify the residential construction process, highlighting the essential components, systems, and sequences that converge to build a home. It serves as a practical guide to understanding the intricacies of constructing a typical residential dwelling.

Effective communication between homeowners and construction professionals is key to the success of any construction project. Here are some tips to ensure clear and productive interactions:

1. **Clearly Define Project Expectations**: Before the project begins, have a detailed discussion about the job's expectations. This includes the scope, timeline, budget, and desired outcomes.
2. **Maintain Regular and Open Communication**: Keep regular and open lines of communication throughout the project. This could be through weekly meetings, email updates, or a shared digital platform where progress can be tracked.
3. **Use Visual Aids and Documentation**: Utilize drawings, plans, and other visual aids to help clarify details. Ensure all changes and agreements are documented to avoid misunderstandings.
4. **Be Open to Questions and Concerns**: Encourage a two-way dialogue where both parties feel comfortable asking questions and raising concerns. This helps to address issues promptly and keep the project on track.
5. **Seek Professional Assistance**: If necessary, don't hesitate to hire a project manager or consultant to facilitate communication and ensure that your interests are represented effectively.

By following these guidelines, homeowners can foster a positive working relationship with their construction team, leading to a smoother project flow and successful outcomes.

When communicating with professionals in the construction industry, it's important to avoid common pitfalls that can lead to misunderstandings and project delays. Here are some key points to keep in mind:

- **Avoid Jargon**: Use clear and simple language. Industry-specific terms can cause confusion if not everyone is familiar with the terminology.
- **Ensure Real-Time Information Access**: Delays in communication can derail project timelines. Make sure all stakeholders have access to the latest updates.
- **Manage Remote Workforce Challenges**: Different time zones and lack of visibility can increase costs and complicate project management. Establish clear protocols for remote communication.
- **Maintain Proper Documentation**: Manual documentation practices can lead to loss of valuable data and instructions. Utilize digital tools to keep records accessible and up to date.
- **Prevent Data Silos**: Ensure that data collected manually is integrated and accessible to all team members to facilitate collaboration.
- **Clarify Roles and Responsibilities**: Misunderstandings often occur when team members are unclear about their roles. Clearly define each person's responsibilities at the outset of the project.

By being aware of these challenges and actively working to address them, you can foster better communication and collaboration on your construction projects.

The construction industry is leveraging several innovative tools and technologies to enhance communication and collaboration. Here are some of the key advancements:

- **Mobile Applications**: Designed for construction teams, these apps enable real-time communication and collaboration from the field.
- **Virtual and Augmented Reality (VR/AR)**: These technologies transform construction processes by providing immersive experiences for training, safety, and project visualization.
- **Cloud-Based Collaboration Platforms**: These platforms facilitate seamless sharing of documents, plans, and updates, ensuring all stakeholders have access to the latest information.
- **Building Information Modeling (BIM)**: BIM software allows for the creation of digital representations of physical and functional characteristics of places, which can be shared across different stakeholders for better decision-making.
- **Construction Robots**: While not directly related to communication, robots increase the accuracy of construction processes and can be remotely monitored and controlled, contributing to better workflow management.

These tools are transforming the way construction projects are managed by improving the efficiency and accuracy of communication, leading to more successful project outcomes.

There are several case studies that highlight the successful implementation of innovative tools and technologies in the construction industry. Here are a few examples:

1. **Building Information Modeling (BIM)**: BIM has been widely adopted for its ability to facilitate better visualization, coordination, and simulation during the construction process. A systematic review found that BIM, often used in combination with other technologies like UAVs/UAS, GIS, LiDAR, and multidimensional modeling, has led to improvements in work efficiency, health and safety, productivity, quality, and sustainability.
2. **Additive Manufacturing (3D Printing)**: The application of 3D printing in construction has shown benefits in waste reduction, design flexibility, constructability, and workforce savings. Case studies have demonstrated its potential in creating complex architectural forms and reducing the carbon footprint of construction activities.
3. **Integration of Construction 4.0 Technologies**: A research study presented a four-layer implementation plan for integrating Construction 4.0 technologies into the industry. The case study showcased how these technologies could be integrated throughout the project lifecycle, improving connectivity and interaction among various construction processes.
4. **Small-Scale Construction Innovations**: Interviews and case studies on small-scale construction projects have provided insights into the implementation of product, tool, and system technologies. These innovations have addressed a cross-section of advances, enhancing the overall construction process.

These case studies demonstrate the transformative impact of technology on the construction industry, leading to more efficient, safe, and sustainable building practices.

PART I: The Forces a Residential Structure is Designed and Built to Withstand

"A house built on granite and strong foundations, not even the onslaught of pouring rain, gushing torrents and strong winds will be able to pull down."

Haile Selassie

Constructing a residential structure is not just about creating a space for living; it's about engineering a safe haven that can endure the forces of nature and the stresses of daily life. This chapter explores the myriad of forces that a typical single-family home is designed to withstand, ensuring the safety and comfort of its occupants.

Dead Loads: The Constant Weight Every structure is subject to its own weight, known as dead loads. These include the mass of walls, floors, roofs, and fixed installations. The structural design must account for these permanent forces to prevent any deformation or collapse.

Live Loads: The Transient Forces Live loads refer to temporary, movable forces exerted by occupants, furniture, vehicles, and even snow on the roof. Residential structures are designed with a margin of safety to accommodate these variable loads without compromising structural integrity.

Environmental Forces: Wind and Weather Wind load is a critical factor in structural design, especially in areas prone to high winds or hurricanes. The force exerted by wind can affect the stability of a structure, necessitating the use of wind-resistant design principles and materials. Weatherproofing measures, such as fluid-applied barriers and sealants, protect against moisture intrusion, which can weaken structural components over time.

Seismic Forces: Earthquakes In seismically active regions, homes must be designed to absorb and dissipate the energy released during an earthquake. This involves the use of flexible materials, seismic bracing, and specially engineered foundations that can move with the ground without causing damage to the structure.

Thermal Forces: Expansion and Contraction Temperature fluctuations cause materials to expand and contract, which can lead to cracks and structural fatigue. To counter this, expansion joints and careful material selection are essential to allow for movement without damaging the home.

Soil and Foundation Forces The foundation bears the entire weight of the structure and transfers it to the ground. It must be designed to handle not only the building's load but also any additional forces from the soil, such as swelling, shrinkage, or erosion. Soil investigations inform the type of foundation used, whether shallow or deep, to ensure stability.

Hydrostatic Forces: Water Pressure Subterranean water can exert hydrostatic pressure on basement walls and foundations. Proper drainage systems, waterproofing, and sump pumps are employed to manage these forces and prevent water damage.

Fire Resistance While not a force in the traditional sense, fire resistance is a critical aspect of residential design. Materials and systems are chosen for their ability to resist and contain fire, providing occupants with time to evacuate and minimizing structural damage.

Residential structures are designed to endure a variety of natural forces to ensure the safety and comfort of their occupants. Understanding these forces is crucial for both builders and homeowners.

Environmental Forces:

1. **Rain**: Structures must have adequate drainage systems to handle precipitation without water intrusion.
2. **Wind**: Buildings are subjected to wind pressures that can cause uplift or suction, necessitating strong connections and anchoring.
3. **Wind-Driven Rain**: Special attention is given to exterior finishes and openings to prevent leakage.
4. **Sun**: The design accounts for the sun's varying positions throughout the year, affecting thermal comfort and lighting.

5. **Snow**: Roof structures must support snow loads, which vary by geographic location.
6. **Seismic Activity**: In earthquake-prone areas, buildings are reinforced to absorb and dissipate seismic energy.
7. **Storms and Natural Disasters**: Construction standards aim to protect structures from extreme weather events as much as possible.

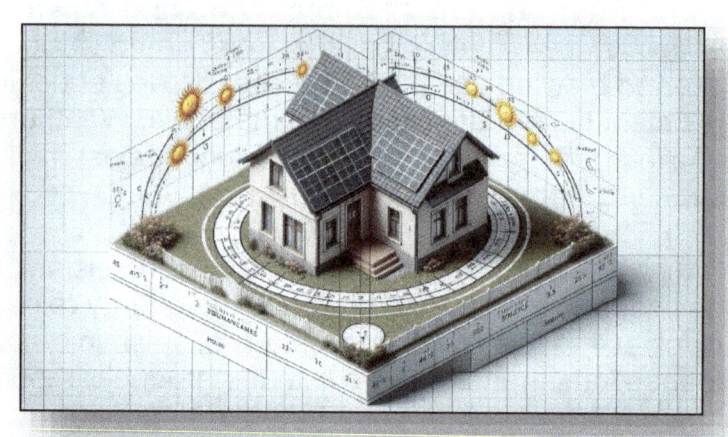

Structural Forces:

- **Wind Pressure**: Buildings are engineered to withstand both uplift and suction forces caused by wind.
- **Ground Pressure**: Foundations are designed to resist hydrostatic pressure and soil movement.
- **Dead Loads**: These include the weight of the structure itself, such as lumber, sheathing, and roofing materials.
- **Live Loads**: Dynamic forces such as the weight of occupants, furniture, and movable objects.

Tendencies Induced by Forces:

- **Racking**: Lateral forces can cause the structure to tilt or distort.
- **Rotation**: Imbalanced forces can lead to a rotational movement.
- **Shear or Slide**: Horizontal forces can cause different parts of the building to move in opposite directions.
- **Lift**: Uplift forces can detach components from the rest of the structure.

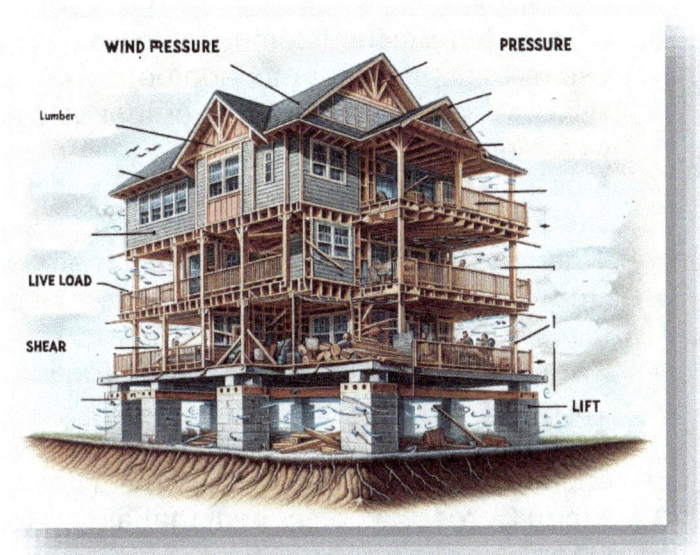

The Four Ds of Building Science:

1. **Deflection**: The ability to redirect water away from the building.
2. **Drainage**: The capacity to eliminate water that infiltrates the building envelope.
3. **Drying**: The ability of materials and assemblies to release absorbed moisture.
4. **Durability**: The longevity of building materials and their resistance to environmental factors.

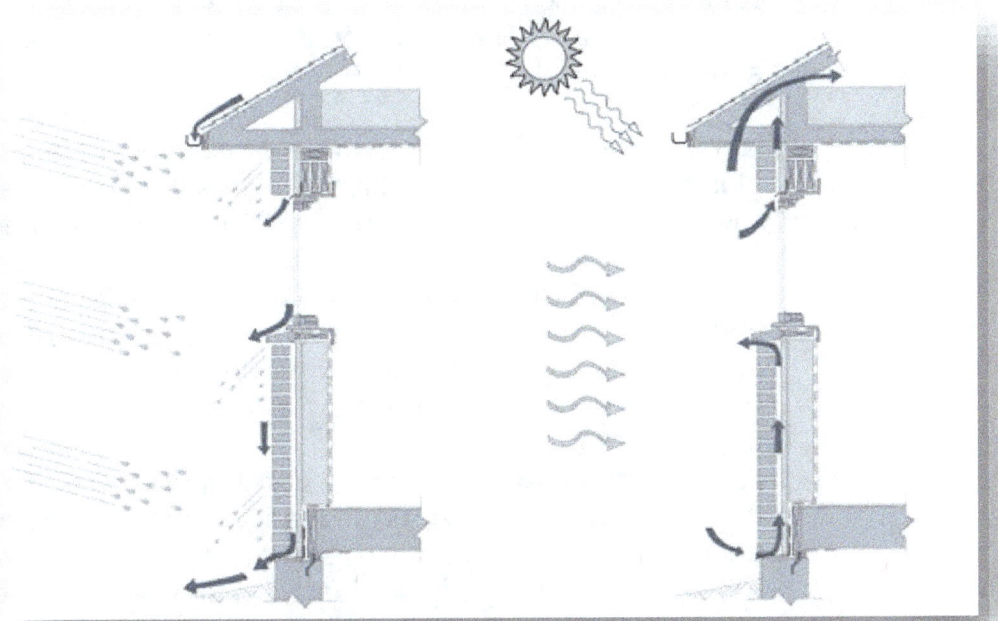

Glossary of Common Terms:

- **Rebar**: A reinforcing bar used to strengthen concrete, measured in eighths of an inch.
- **WWM**: Welded wire mesh, similar to rebar, used for reinforcing concrete.

- **Post-Tension Slab**: A technique where concrete is pre-stressed to enhance strength and span capabilities.
- **Hold-Down**: Hardware providing resistance to uplift forces on walls.
- **Concealed Barrier**: Components like WRB and flashing that are hidden but essential for moisture management.
- **WRB**: Weather-resistant barrier that acts as a secondary defense against water intrusion.
- **Flashing**: Materials that ensure continuity with the WRB and facilitate water shedding.
- **Waterproofing**: The application of materials to prevent water penetration.
- **Underlayment**: A layer between the roof deck and shingles or tiles that serves as a secondary weather barrier.
- **Composition Shingle**: A common roofing material made of asphalt, felt, fiberglass, and granules.
- **Concrete Tile**: Roofing tiles made of concrete, available in various profiles and colors.
- **Weep Screed**: A component that allows for drainage at the base of stucco walls.
- **Z-Bar**: A flashing piece used at horizontal terminations, such as the top of a stucco wall.
- **Head Wall**: The junction where a sloped roof meets a vertical wall.
- **Confined Rake**: The edge detail where a roof plane transitions to a vertical surface.

Builders are required to adhere to a set of industry standards that ensure the safety, durability, and efficiency of residential structures. These standards are established and regulated by various authoritative organizations:

- **International Code Council (ICC)**: The ICC develops model codes that serve as the foundation for building codes adopted and enforced by jurisdictions worldwide. These codes are updated triennially and are integral to the legal framework of construction.

- **American Society for Testing and Materials (ASTM)**: The ASTM is a globally recognized leader in the development and delivery of voluntary consensus standards. It covers a wide range of materials, products, systems, and services used in construction.

- **American Architectural Manufacturers Association (AAMA)**: The AAMA sets performance standards for windows, doors, and other fenestration products to ensure high quality and durability.
- **American Concrete Institute (ACI)**: The ACI is a leading authority on concrete technology and develops standards, technical resources, educational programs, and certifications for individuals and organizations involved in concrete design, construction, and materials.

- **The Engineered Wood Association (APA)**: The APA provides quality auditing and testing, research, and market support for engineered wood products.
- **Construction Specifications Institute (CSI)**: See below.

Construction Spécifications Institute (CSI) Construction Divisions

This section provides an overview of the Construction Specifications Institute (CSI) and its role in standardizing construction specifications through the MasterFormat. We will explore the divisions of construction as defined by CSI, which serve as a framework for organizing construction information.

The Evolution of CSI Divisions

In the early days of construction project management, the industry lacked a standardized system for organizing specifications, leading to confusion and inefficiency. Recognizing the need for uniformity, the Construction Specifications Institute (CSI) was founded in 1948 and began to address this issue. By 1963, CSI had published a format for construction specifications that introduced 16 major divisions of work. This system, known as MasterFormat, provided a master list of divisions and section numbers and titles within each division to follow in organizing information about a facility's construction requirements and associated activities.

The original 16 divisions were designed to cover all facets of construction work, from general requirements to electrical systems, ensuring that every detail of a construction project could be categorized and referenced efficiently. This standardization improved communication among all parties involved in construction projects, from architects and engineers to contractors and suppliers. The divisions facilitated project planning and execution by providing a clear framework for specifying materials, workmanship, and quality of work. As a result, MasterFormat became the most widely used standard for organizing specifications and other written information for commercial and institutional building projects in the U.S. and Canada.

The success of the 16 divisions lay in their ability to provide a common language for the construction industry, which greatly enhanced the clarity and coordination of project planning and execution. By 2004, the system had evolved to include 50 divisions, reflecting the growth and complexity of the construction industry. However, the origins of the 16 divisions remain a testament to the foresight of the CSI and its commitment to improving the construction process through standardization.

Here is a list of all 50 CSI divisions in order:

- Division 00 - Procurement and Contracting Requirements
- Division 01 - General Requirements
- Division 02 - Existing Conditions

- Division 03 – Concrete - Cast-in-Place Concrete, Precast Concrete, Cast-in-Place Concrete, Structural Framing, Precast Structural Concrete, Concrete Finishing, Concrete Accessories, Concrete Reinforcement.

- Division 04 - Masonry - Masonry Units and Accessories, Masonry Mortaring, Stone Masonry, Manufactured Stone.

- Division 05 - Metals - Structural Metal Framing, Metal Decking, Cold-Formed Metal Framing, Metal Fabrications, Metal Railings, Ornamental Metal, Metal Stairs.

- Division 06 - Wood, Plastics, and Composites - Rough Carpentry, Sheathing, Wood Decking, Structural Plastics, Finish Carpentry, Architectural Woodwork, Composite Fabrications

- Division 07 - Thermal and Moisture Protection - Dampproofing and Waterproofing, Thermal Insulation, Fire and Smoke Protection, Joint Sealants, Expansion Control

- Division 08 – Openings - Hollow Metal Doors and Frames, Wood Doors, Plastic Doors, Hardware, Glazing, Storefronts, Curtain Walls

- Division 09 – Finishes - Plaster and Gypsum Board, Tile, Terrazzo, Flooring, Wall Finishes, Ceilings, Stucco

- Division 10 – Specialties - Information Specialties, Fire Protection Specialties, Security and Safety Specialties, Postal Specialties

- Division 11 – Equipment - Vehicle and Pedestrian Equipment, Loading Dock Equipment, Detention Equipment, Theater and Stage Equipment

- Division 12 - Furnishings - Furniture, Furnishings, Accessories

- Division 13 - Special Construction - Special Purpose Rooms, Special Structures, Integrated Construction

- Division 14 - Conveying Equipment - Elevators, Escalators, Moving Walks, Lifts

- Division 21 - Fire Suppression - Sprinkler Systems, Fire Suppression, Standpipes, Fire Pumps

- Division 22 – Plumbing - Plumbing Equipment, Plumbing Fixtures, Facility Water Distribution, Facility Sewerage and Drainage

- Division 23 - Heating, Ventilating, and Air Conditioning (HVAC) - HVAC Equipment, HVAC Air Distribution, HVAC Fans and Blowers, HVAC Air Cleaning

- Division 24 - Reserved for Future Expansion

- Division 25 - Integrated Automation - Integrated Automation Instrumentation and Terminal Devices, Integrated Automation Control

- Division 26 – Electrical - Electrical Service, Electrical Power Generation, Electrical Power Transmission, Electrical Distribution, Electrical Wiring and Raceways, Electrical Equipment

- Division 27 – Communications - Structured Cabling, Distributed Communications and Monitoring Systems

- Division 28 - Electronic Safety and Security - Electronic Safety and Security Equipment, Electronic Access Control, and Intrusion

- Division 31 – Earthwork - Earth Moving, Excavating, Grading, Waterway Excavation and Containment

- Division 32 - Exterior Improvements - Exterior Improvements, Exterior Protection

- Division 33 – Utilities - Utilities, Water Utility Distribution, Electrical Utility Transmission and Distribution, Gas and Vapor Utility Distribution

- Division 34 – Transportation - Transportation Signaling and Control Equipment, Transportation Equipment

- Division 35 - Waterway and Marine Construction - Waterway Construction and Equipment, Marine Construction and Equipment

- Division 40 - Process Interconnections - Process Integration, Process Instrumentation

- Division 41 - Material Processing and Handling Equipment - Material Processing and Handling Equipment

- Division 42 - Process Heating, Cooling, and Drying Equipment - Process Heating Equipment, Process Cooling Equipment, Process Drying

- Division 43 - Process Gas and Liquid Handling, Purification, and Storage Equipment - Process Gas Handling Equipment, Process Liquid Handling Equipment, Process Purification Equipment, Process Gas and Liquid Storage

- Division 44 - Pollution Control Equipment - Pollution and Waste Control Equipment
- Division 45 - Industry-Specific Manufacturing Equipment - Industry-Specific Manufacturing Equipment
- Division 46 - Water and Wastewater Equipment - Water and Wastewater Equipment
- Division 47 – Reserved for Future Expansion
- Division 48 - Electrical Power Generation
- Division 49 - Electrical Transmission and Distribution -
- Division 50 – Specialized Construction - Specialized Construction

The divisions are designed to cover all facets of construction work and are used to organize specifications and other construction documentation for commercial building projects. They are part of the MasterFormat, which is a standard for organizing specifications and other written information for commercial and institutional building projects in the U.S. and Canada.

The CSI divisions can be incredibly useful for your construction projects in several ways:

1. Project Planning: Use the divisions as a checklist to ensure all aspects of the project are considered during the planning phase. This can help in identifying all the materials, systems, and standards that will be required.

2. Specification Writing: When writing specifications for a project, the divisions provide a structured format. This ensures that all parties involved have a clear understanding of what is required for each part of the construction process.

3. Cost Estimation: The divisions can be used to organize cost estimates. By breaking down the project into smaller parts, it becomes easier to estimate the costs associated with each division, leading to more accurate overall project cost estimations.

4. Quality Control: During the construction process, the divisions can serve as a guide for quality control checks. Each division outlines standards and specifications that need to be met, which can be used to ensure the work is being performed to the required standards.

5. Communication: They provide a common language for all stakeholders involved in a construction project. By referring to the specific division,

everyone can be on the same page about which part of the project is being discussed.

6. Forensic Analysis: In the field of construction forensics, the divisions can be used to categorize and investigate construction defects or failures. By understanding which division a problem falls under, you can more easily identify the cause and suggest remedies.

7. Education and Training: For new employees or team members, the divisions can be a part of educational materials to help them understand the scope of construction projects and the various components they will be working with.

8. Documentation and Record-Keeping: The divisions can help in organizing project documentation, making it easier to find and reference specific documents related to different parts of the construction process.

Understanding the Evolution of Building Codes: Building codes are dynamic; they evolve to incorporate new technologies, materials, and safety practices. For instance, California's Title 24 energy standards have undergone several revisions to improve energy efficiency in buildings:

- The 1998 California Title 24 Energy Standards set the precedent for energy conservation in construction.
- Subsequent updates in 2001, 2005, and 2008 reflected advancements in energy-efficient technologies and practices.

Key Considerations for Compliance: Builders must consider various factors to ensure compliance:

- Determine the specific code under which a project was permitted.
- Recognize if a project spans multiple phases that may be subject to different codes.
- Be aware of any special city ordinances or regional requirements that may apply.

Staying Current with Manufacturer Specifications: Manufacturers' specifications can change, impacting installation requirements. For example, James Hardie's Hardie Panel now necessitates a 3/8" rain screen behind the panel system, affecting the detailing of the assembly with components like insect screening, flashings, and panel supports.

Regional Building Practices: Construction methods vary by region due to factors such as climate and local expertise:

- In the Pacific Northwest, structures are typically "dried in" before interior work commences.
- In the Southeast, construction often begins with CMU blocks or poured concrete.
- Hawaiian builders commonly use chemically preserved lumber due to the island's climate.

Compliance with industry standards is not just a legal requirement; it's a commitment to quality and safety. By staying informed and adaptable, builders can navigate the complexities of these standards and deliver residential structures that stand the test of time.

Builders can ensure compliance with industry standards during construction by adopting a comprehensive approach that includes the following steps:

1. **Learn the Basic Regulatory Compliance Requirements**: Familiarize yourself with the regulations that apply to your business, such as building codes, insurance and bonding requirements, safety regulations, and more.
2. **Reduce Manual Compliance Processes**: Make sure all relevant personnel are aware of the compliance requirements. Implement digital tools to streamline the tracking and management of compliance documentation.
3. **Stay Organized with Dedicated Construction Compliance Solutions**: Utilize construction compliance software to keep track of budgets, deadlines, change orders, progress reports, payroll, safety, and compliance requirements.
4. **Regular Training for Staff**: Provide ongoing education to ensure that all team members are up to date on the latest standards and best practices.
5. **Appoint a Compliance Officer**: Have a dedicated individual or team responsible for overseeing adherence to regulations and handling all compliance-related documentation.
6. **Stay Updated on Changes**: Regulations can change, so it's important to stay informed about any updates or revisions to the standards that affect your projects.
7. **Implement ISO Standards**: Consider obtaining ISO certification, such as ISO 9001 for quality management or ISO 45001 for occupational health and safety, to demonstrate compliance with international standards.

By following these steps, builders can maintain compliance throughout the construction process, thereby minimizing risks and ensuring the safety and legality of their projects.

Non-compliance with industry standards can have serious repercussions on the safety and performance of a residential structure. Here are some examples:

- **Personal Protective Equipment (PPE) Non-Compliance**: Failure to provide and enforce the use of PPE like hard hats, safety glasses, gloves, and boots can lead to accidents and injuries on the construction site.

- **Equipment Maintenance**: Neglecting the proper maintenance of equipment, tools, and machinery can result in malfunctions that may cause accidents, potentially harming workers and compromising the structural integrity of the building.
- **Safety Inspections**: Skipping regular safety inspections or ignoring identified hazards can lead to unsafe working conditions and increase the risk of structural failures due to unaddressed issues.
- **Building Codes**: Not adhering to building codes can result in structures that are not resilient against environmental stresses such as wind, seismic activity, or heavy snow loads, posing a risk to occupants and property.
- **Environmental Regulations**: Ignoring environmental regulations can lead to improper handling of hazardous materials, which can contaminate the site and pose health risks to workers and future residents.

These examples illustrate the importance of compliance with industry standards to ensure the safety of workers during construction and the long-term performance and safety of the residential structure.

Non-compliance with construction standards has led to several notable structural failures and safety incidents in residential buildings. Here are a few real-world cases:

- **Champlain Towers South Collapse**: In June 2021, the partial collapse of the Champlain Towers South condominium in Surfside, Florida, resulted in significant loss of life. The disaster highlighted the potential consequences of structural damage and corrosion of foundational elements.
- **Harbour Cay Condominium Collapse**: In March 1981, the Harbour Cay Condominium in Cocoa Beach, Florida, collapsed during construction due to multiple design and construction flaws, including insufficient shear capacity. This led to more rigorous enforcement of building codes in Florida and nationwide.
- **Hyatt Regency Walkway Collapse**: In July 1981, the collapse of skywalks at the Hyatt Regency Hotel in Kansas City, Missouri, killed 114 people and injured more than 200. The incident was attributed to design flaws and led to significant changes in engineering standards and practices.

These cases underscore the critical importance of adhering to industry standards and regulations to ensure the safety and integrity of residential structures. Compliance with these standards is essential to prevent such tragedies and protect the lives of occupants and construction workers.

Builders can learn from past incidents and prevent similar failures in the future by adopting several key practices:

1. **Study Past Failures**: Analyze case studies and reports of past construction failures to understand the root causes and contributing factors.

2. **Implement a Culture of Safety**: Prioritize safety over speed or cost savings, ensuring that all decisions are made with the well-being of workers and future occupants in mind.
3. **Continual Education**: Engage in ongoing education programs, workshops, and seminars that focus on best practices, new technologies, and lessons learned from past failures.
4. **Risk Assessment**: Incorporate comprehensive risk assessments into the planning and execution of projects to identify potential issues early on.
5. **Quality Assurance and Control**: Establish rigorous quality assurance and control processes to ensure that construction meets or exceeds industry standards.
6. **Collaboration and Communication**: Foster open communication among all stakeholders, including engineers, architects, contractors, and workers, to ensure that concerns are addressed promptly.
7. **Adherence to Codes and Standards**: Stay updated on the latest building codes and industry standards and ensure strict adherence to these guidelines throughout the construction process.

By integrating these practices into their operations, builders can significantly reduce the risk of structural failures and enhance the overall safety and quality of their projects.

Chapter One: Planning and Development

"By failing to prepare, you are preparing to fail."

Benjamin Franklin

Introduction to Planning and Development: The initial phase of any construction project involves meticulous planning and development. This chapter outlines the key considerations and steps in the process, ensuring a solid foundation for the subsequent construction stages.

Key Considerations:

- **Construction Type**: The choice of construction type is dictated by the intended use of the building and the level of fire protection required. This ranges from Type I-A for high-rise buildings to Type V-B for single-family homes.
- **Zoning Restrictions**: Zoning codes regulate how a structure integrates into its community, affecting various aspects such as setbacks, usage, and design.
- **Plot Divisions**: Proper division of the site into plots is crucial for organized development and efficient use of space.
- **Microclimate Conditions**: Local environmental conditions influence construction methods and material choices.

- **Final Aesthetics**: The visual impact of the structure, including cladding types, must align with community standards and bylaws.

Constructing a residential house is a multifaceted process that involves careful planning and development through various stages. This chapter will explore the key aspects of these stages, including construction types, zoning restrictions, plot divisions, microclimate conditions, and final aesthetics.

Construction Types Residential construction can be classified into several types based on the International Residential Code (IRC), which includes Type I through Type V constructions. These types range from fire-resistive structures to wood-framed buildings, each with different fire-resistance ratings and construction materials.

Zoning Restrictions Zoning laws play a crucial role in residential construction, dictating land use, building types, and other regulations to ensure compatibility and functionality within a community. These laws can affect everything from the height and footprint of a house to the allowable activities within its premises.

Plot Divisions Dividing land into smaller plots for development is governed by local regulations and can impact the layout and size of residential properties. Proper adherence to these regulations is essential for legal compliance and the successful subdivision of property for residential use.

Microclimate Conditions The microclimate of a construction site can significantly influence the design and sustainability of a house. Factors such as topography, vegetation, and water bodies can affect temperature, humidity, and overall comfort. Architects must consider these conditions to create energy-efficient and comfortable homes.

Final Aesthetics The final aesthetics of a residential house encompass the visual appeal and design harmony of the structure. This includes the selection of materials, colors, finishes, and architectural details that contribute to the overall beauty and character of the home.

Understanding Construction Types: Construction types are categorized based on fire resistance and material use, each suited to different building specifications and safety requirements.

Navigating Zoning Restrictions: Zoning codes are designed to maintain harmony within the community. Builders must navigate these regulations, which vary by district and can influence the project's design and functionality.

Adapting to Microclimate Conditions: Builders must adapt their practices to local environmental conditions, such as wind loads and snowfall, which can significantly affect the structural integrity and performance of the building.

Achieving Final Aesthetics: The final appearance of a structure is often governed by local bylaws. Architectural renderings and adherence to aesthetic guidelines are typically required for permitting.

Construction Activities and Phases: The construction site is organized into plots, with each phase carefully planned. This includes identifying the appropriate home plan for each lot and incorporating necessary variations to maintain architectural diversity.

Estimated Construction Duration: The construction process, from architectural drawings to final review, is estimated to take approximately 13 months, though this can vary based on project complexity and scale.

This chapter provides an overview of the essential elements of planning and development in residential construction. Adherence to these guidelines ensures a project's success from the ground up.

Zoning restrictions play a significant role in shaping the design and layout of residential developments. Here are some examples of how these restrictions can impact construction projects:

- **Material Use**: Zoning regulations may prohibit or limit the use of certain exterior materials, such as vinyl siding and metal, and may require specific, often more expensive materials for siding and fences.
- **Building Massing**: Zoning laws can dictate the massing of buildings, influencing their height, shape, and the overall density of the development.
- **Land Use**: Zoning can restrict the types of activities allowed on a property, such as limiting commercial or industrial uses in residential zones.
- **Historic Preservation**: In historic districts, zoning may impose overlays or design restrictions that dictate the architectural features of new constructions, including the types of windows and doors that can be used.
- **Environmental Considerations**: Properties with environmental sensitivities, such as wetlands or habitats for endangered species, may face additional zoning restrictions that impact development plans.

These examples illustrate how zoning laws influence various aspects of residential development, from the choice of building materials to the overall design and functionality of the neighborhood. Adhering to these regulations is crucial for the successful planning and execution of construction projects.

Builders can proactively address zoning restrictions during the initial design phase by implementing the following measures:

1. **Early Engagement with Zoning Authorities**: Reach out to local zoning offices early in the planning process to understand the specific regulations and obtain guidance on necessary permits.
2. **Thorough Research**: Conduct comprehensive research on the zoning laws that apply to the project's location, including land use, density, height restrictions, and environmental considerations.
3. **Professional Consultation**: Work with architects, planners, and legal experts who are well-versed in local zoning codes to ensure that the initial designs comply with all regulations.
4. **Community Involvement**: Engage with the community and local officials to gain insights into potential zoning changes and community expectations.
5. **Flexible Design Strategies**: Create adaptable design plans that can be easily modified to accommodate potential zoning changes or variances.
6. **Regular Updates**: Stay informed about any changes to zoning laws that may occur during the design phase and adjust plans accordingly.

By taking these proactive steps, builders can minimize the risk of costly revisions and ensure a smoother, more efficient construction process.

Here are examples where early consideration of zoning regulations contributed to streamlined development processes:

- **Urban Land Institute Report**: A report by the Urban Land Institute highlighted how updating zoning policies can support health, social equity, and climate action. It shared examples of zoning policy innovations from across the United States that have led to increased production of a variety of housing types and more affordable housing.
- **Flexible Zoning in Housing Affordability**: Research by the Brookings Institution and Harvard's Joint Center for Housing Studies found that flexible zoning and streamlined procedures can make housing more affordable. By allowing developers more flexibility in land use and reducing procedural barriers, building apartments becomes less expensive, demonstrating the benefits of early zoning consideration.

These examples show that when zoning regulations are considered early in the planning process, they can lead to more efficient and cost-effective development projects.

Innovative design solutions have been instrumental in addressing complex zoning challenges in urban areas. Here are some examples:

- **Mixed-Use Zoning**: Cities are promoting mixed-use zoning to allow for a combination of residential, commercial, and recreational spaces within a given area. This approach helps create balanced environments where residents can conveniently access essential services.
- **Inclusionary Zoning**: Some urban areas implement inclusionary zoning to encourage the development of affordable housing within new residential

projects. This policy often requires a certain percentage of units to be set aside for low- to moderate-income households.
- **Infrastructure Improvements**: Investing in infrastructure improvements, such as public transportation and pedestrian-friendly streetscapes, supports the development of compact, mixed-use communities. This can lead to a shift toward transit, biking, and walking, reducing reliance on cars.
- **Zoning for Health, Sustainability, and Resilience**: Updating zoning policies to support health, social equity, and climate action can increase the likelihood that development reflects locally defined priorities. For example, providing parks and open space viewed as critical infrastructure.

The planning and development phases of constructing a residential house require a comprehensive understanding of various factors that influence the final outcome. By considering construction types, zoning restrictions, plot divisions, microclimate conditions, and aesthetics, developers and architects can ensure the creation of a functional, compliant, and visually appealing residence.

Chapter Two: Infrastructure, Site Preparation & Grading

"We protect nature not for nature's sake but for our own sake because it's the infrastructure of our communities."

Robert F. Kennedy, Jr.

Constructing a residential house is a complex endeavor that requires meticulous planning and execution during various stages. This chapter will delve into the intricacies of infrastructure coordination and installation, site preparation, grading, and other critical aspects that contribute to the successful construction of a residential house.

Infrastructure Coordination and Installation The success of a residential development hinges on the seamless integration of various infrastructure systems. These include utilities, digital infrastructure, transportation, and community facilities. Effective coordination with developers, municipal officials, and third-party intermediaries is essential to align these systems with the broader goals of economic mobility and community development.

Site Preparation and Grading Site preparation is the foundational step in construction, involving surveying, ground clearing, excavation, grading, and compaction. It ensures that the ground is structurally sound to support the building, its systems, and occupants. Grading involves modifying the land's contours to manage water flow and establish a level base for construction.

Construction Site Activities Managing a construction site effectively is crucial for the quality of the finished product. It involves a myriad of activities such as material delivery, plan execution, and issue resolution. Safety, security, and efficiency are paramount, with considerations for traffic control, material staging, and waste management.

Soils Inspection, Analysis, and Reports A comprehensive understanding of soil properties is vital for determining the suitability of the site for construction. Soil testing reports provide insights into nutrient content, pH levels, and potential contaminants, guiding decisions on land use and necessary amendments for optimal building conditions.

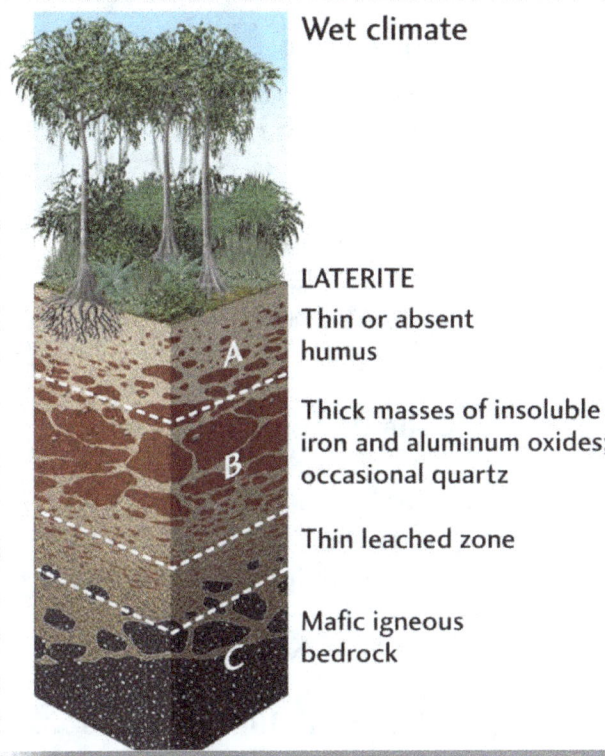

Collaborations with City and County Regulations Navigating the regulatory landscape is a critical component of residential construction. Collaborations between cities and counties can facilitate the adherence to state and federal mandates, grant-based incentives, and local guidelines, ensuring compliance and fostering economic mobility.

Microclimate Conditions Microclimate conditions significantly influence the design and sustainability of a house. Factors such as topography, vegetation, surface materials, and water bodies must be considered to create energy-efficient and comfortable homes that are resilient to climate change and extreme weather events.

Final Aesthetics The final aesthetics of a residential house are shaped by numerous design decisions made throughout the construction process. These include choices of materials, colors, finishes, and architectural details that enhance the visual appeal and ensure the building complements its context.

Essential Considerations:

- **Soils Report**: A comprehensive soils report is crucial for understanding the geotechnical properties of the site, which informs decisions on foundation design and necessary site modifications.

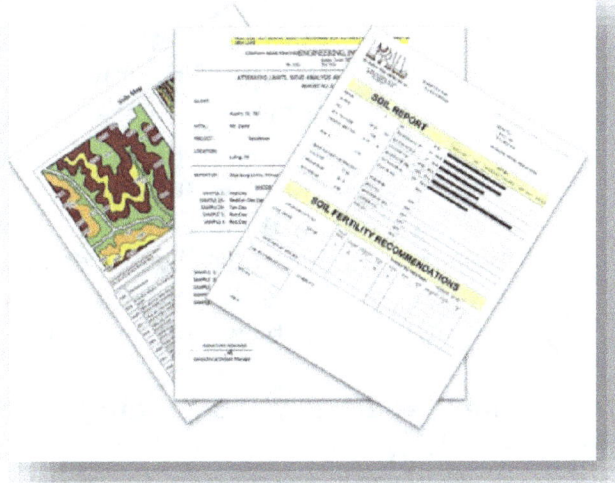

Infrastructure Coordination:

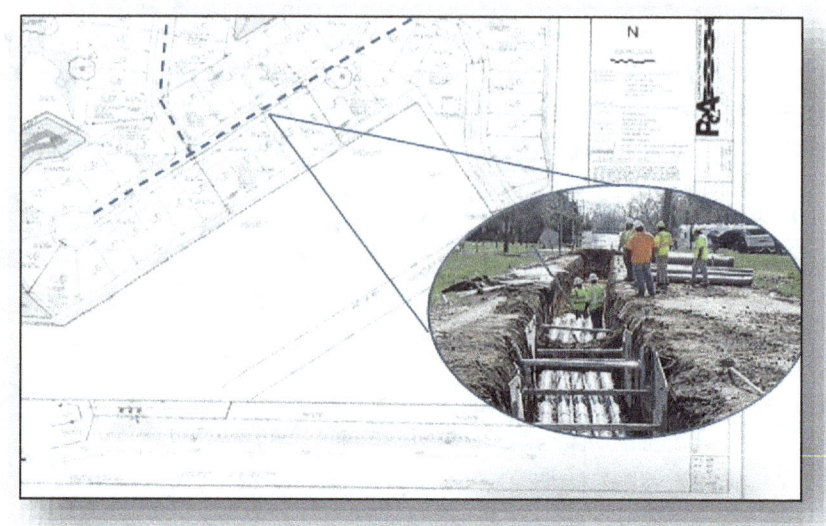

- **City Collaboration**: Effective coordination with city services is essential for the installation of main site infrastructure, including sewers, water, electricity, streets, and lighting.

The Soils Engineering Report:

- **Soil Analysis**: Identifying soil types and expansion rates, along with detecting any toxic or hazardous substances, is vital for safe and sustainable construction practices.

Construction Activities:

- **Infrastructure Installation**: The city typically installs primary infrastructure such as sewers, water, gas, and electrical lines, followed by streets, curbs, street lighting, and sidewalks.
    - **Vision Clearance**: Ensuring clear sightlines at intersections for safety.
    - **Intersection Design**: Properly angled intersections to facilitate traffic flow.
    - **Lighting Design**: Strategically placed street lighting for visibility and security.

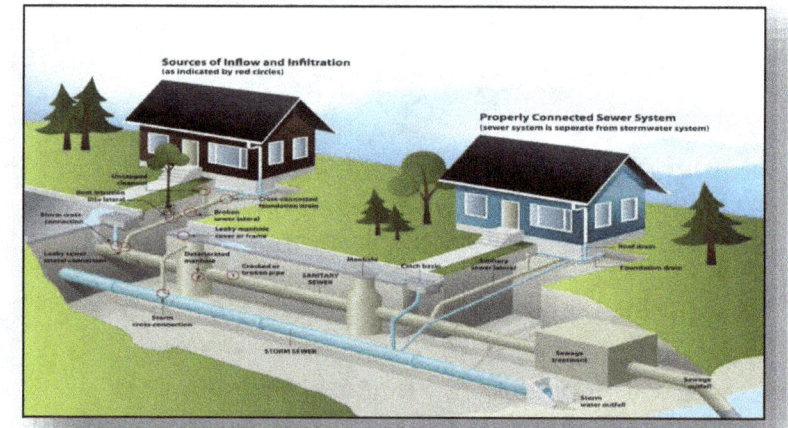

Site Preparation and Grading:

- **Grading Process**: Once plans are approved, grading begins to shape the land according to design specifications.

- **Soil Management**: Removal of debris and unsuitable soils, followed by the addition of clean fill to achieve a level base with appropriate drainage.
- **Contour Mapping**: Utilizing contour maps to guide the grading process and ensure proper land shaping.

Estimated Construction Duration:

- Approximately 20 days for:
    - Clearing and rough grading of the lot.
    - Establishing temporary power.
    - Laying underground utilities.

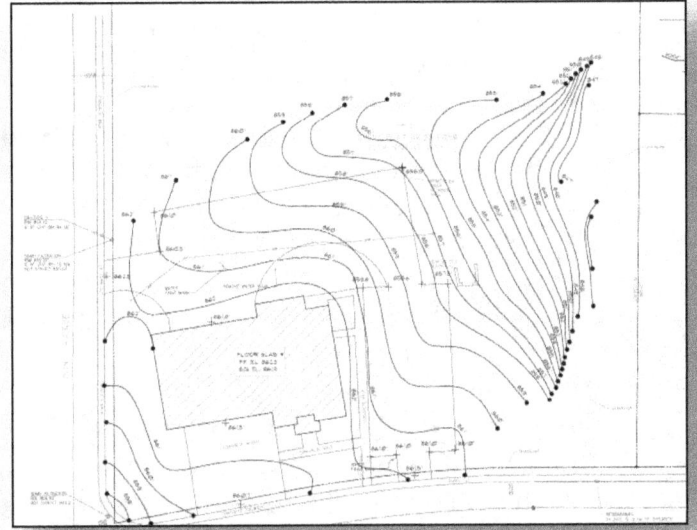

Builders can effectively manage soil-related challenges during site preparation by implementing several strategies:

1. **Conduct a Comprehensive Soils Report**: Before construction begins, perform a detailed analysis of the soil to identify its type, expansion rates, and any toxic or hazardous chemicals present.
2. **Erosion and Sedimentation Control**: Implement measures to prevent soil erosion and manage sedimentation, such as silt fences, sediment basins, and erosion control blankets.
3. **Soil Stabilization**: Use techniques like compaction, geotextiles, or chemical stabilization to increase soil strength and stability.
4. **Proper Drainage**: Ensure adequate drainage systems are in place to manage water flow and prevent soil erosion and instability.
5. **Use of Suitable Fill Material**: Bring in clean fill material to create a level surface and ensure proper compaction and drainage.
6. **Revegetation**: As soon as possible, establish vegetation to protect the soil from erosion and help stabilize the site.

By following these steps, builders can address soil-related challenges effectively, ensuring a stable foundation for construction and minimizing the risk of future problems.

Builders can collaborate with geotechnical engineers to optimize soil management during site preparation by:

1. **Engaging Early**: Involve geotechnical engineers from the project's outset to benefit from their expertise in soil analysis and foundation design.

2. **Sharing Information**: Provide the geotechnical team with detailed project plans and any previous soil reports to ensure they have a comprehensive understanding of the site conditions.
3. **Conducting Thorough Soil Investigations**: Work closely with geotechnical engineers to conduct extensive soil testing and analysis, which will inform the design and construction approach.
4. **Designing Foundations Based on Soil Conditions**: Utilize the geotechnical engineer's recommendations to design foundations that are appropriate for the soil conditions, whether that involves standard footings, piers, or specialized systems.
5. **Implementing Soil Stabilization Techniques**: Collaborate on selecting and applying the most effective soil stabilization methods, such as compaction, the use of geotextiles, or chemical treatments, to improve soil bearing capacity and reduce settlement.
6. **Addressing Environmental Impact**: Ensure that soil management strategies align with environmental regulations and sustainability goals, with guidance from geotechnical engineers on practices like erosion control and sediment management.
7. **Regular Communication and Updates**: Maintain open lines of communication throughout the project to address any unforeseen soil-related issues promptly and effectively.

By fostering a collaborative relationship with geotechnical engineers, builders can ensure that soil management is handled effectively, reducing the risk of costly delays, and ensuring the stability and longevity of the construction project.

The choice of foundation type has a significant impact on soil management strategies during site preparation. Here's how different foundation types can influence the approach:

- **Shallow Foundations**: For soils with good bearing capacity, shallow foundations like slab-on-grade or spread footings are used. Soil management involves ensuring uniformity in soil strength and compaction to prevent differential settlement.
- **Deep Foundations**: In areas with poor soil conditions, deep foundations such as piles or caissons are necessary. Soil management strategies include extensive testing to determine the depth required to reach stable soil and may involve the removal of unstable soil layers.
- **Mat Foundations**: When the load is distributed over a large area, mat or raft foundations are chosen. Soil management includes grading and compaction to create a level base that can support the broader foundation structure.
- **Specialized Foundations**: In cases of expansive soils or other challenging conditions, specialized foundations like drilled piers or grade beams may be used. Soil management must address issues like swelling, shrinkage, and drainage to ensure the foundation's integrity.

Each foundation type requires a tailored approach to soil management to ensure the long-term stability and safety of the structure.

Innovative foundation designs have been developed to address challenging soil conditions while minimizing environmental impact. Here are some examples:

1. **Disaggregated Models for Sustainability**: Researchers have proposed disaggregated models to evaluate the sustainability of foundations, focusing on soil improvement and construction methods. These models consider transportation of materials, worker commute, construction process, and emissions of dust, noise, and vibrations.
2. **Sustainable Foundation Design and Construction**: Conferences like GeoMandu discuss sustainable foundation designs that address challenging soil conditions. Topics include ground improvement techniques for earthquake-resilient structures and innovative foundation design for sustainable infrastructure.
3. **Helical Piles and Lightweight Aggregate**: Innovations in foundation design, such as helical piles and lightweight aggregate fill materials, offer potential for cost-effective solutions that are less invasive and reduce the use of concrete.
4. **Beyond Concrete Techniques**: Engineers are exploring materials and techniques beyond traditional concrete for foundation design. These innovative approaches allow for optimization of foundation performance in challenging soil conditions without extensive excavation or reinforcements.

These examples highlight the ongoing efforts to develop foundation designs that are both effective in complex soil environments and mindful of their environmental footprint.

Chapter Summary/Key Takeaways

Summary of Chapter Two: Infrastructure, Site Preparation, and Grading

- **Soils Report**: Essential for determining foundation requirements and addressing potential soil contaminants.
- **City Collaboration**: Coordination with municipal services is key for installing essential infrastructure.
- **Soil Analysis**: Critical for safe construction and environmental sustainability.
- **Infrastructure Installation**: Includes the setup of sewer, water, gas, electrical lines, and roadworks.
- **Grading Process**: Involves shaping the land, managing soil quality, and ensuring proper drainage.
- **Construction Duration**: Site preparation typically takes around 20 days, including grading and utility setup.

Key Takeaways:

- A thorough understanding of soil conditions and proactive collaboration with city services streamline the site preparation phase.
- Effective soil management and grading are fundamental to laying a solid foundation for construction.
- Adhering to a well-planned schedule ensures timely completion of this crucial stage.

The planning and development phases of constructing a residential house encompass a broad range of activities that require careful consideration and coordination. By addressing infrastructure needs, preparing the site, adhering to regulations, considering microclimate conditions, and focusing on aesthetics, developers can ensure the creation of a functional, compliant, and visually appealing residence.

PART II: Construction

"May you have a strong foundation when the winds of change shift... and may you be forever young."

    Bob Dylan

Building Dreams into Reality

The world of residential construction is a dynamic field that combines art, science, and business. It's where dreams are translated into tangible structures—homes that provide shelter, comfort, and a canvas for family memories.

The Foundation of Residential Construction

At its core, residential construction is about creating spaces where life unfolds. It's a process that begins with an idea and evolves through design, planning, and meticulous execution. The industry has seen a significant transformation with the integration of sustainable practices and advanced technologies, making homes not only more efficient but also more harmonious with the environment.

Designing for the Future

Today's residential construction is not just about building four walls and a roof: it's about envisioning a future. Architects and builders work closely to design homes that are both aesthetically pleasing and functional. They consider factors like natural light, space utilization, and energy efficiency, ensuring that the final product is a home that stands the test of time.

Sustainability: A Cornerstone of Modern Construction

Sustainability has become a cornerstone of residential construction. Homeowners are increasingly aware of their environmental footprint, seeking out eco-friendly materials and energy-saving features. From solar panels to rainwater harvesting systems, the modern home is designed to reduce waste and promote a greener lifestyle.

The Role of Technology

Technology has revolutionized residential construction. With tools like 3D modeling and Building Information Modeling (BIM), builders can create detailed plans and virtual walkthroughs before the first brick is laid. This not only improves accuracy but also allows for better communication with clients, ensuring their vision is perfectly captured.

Navigating the Construction Process

The construction process can be complex, involving various stages from site preparation to the final touches. Each phase requires careful planning and coordination, often involving a team of professionals including engineers, contractors, and interior designers. The goal is to create a seamless flow of work that adheres to timelines and budgets while maintaining high-quality standards.

Challenges and Solutions

Residential construction faces its share of challenges, from zoning restrictions to material shortages. However, the industry is adept at finding solutions, whether it's through innovative design to maximize space in urban areas or utilizing new materials that offer durability and cost-effectiveness.

Building Communities

Beyond individual homes, residential construction plays a pivotal role in shaping communities. It's about creating neighborhoods that foster connection, with shared spaces and amenities that bring people together. The design of a community can have a profound impact on the quality of life for its residents, influencing everything from social interaction to physical well-being.

Residential construction is an ever-evolving field that reflects the changing needs and desires of society. It's a blend of creativity and practicality, resulting in homes that are more than just structures—they're the backdrop to our lives. As we look to the future, the industry continues to innovate, ensuring that the homes we build today will be cherished for generations to come.

In conclusion, residential construction is not just about erecting buildings; it's about crafting environments that enhance our daily experiences. It's a testament to human ingenuity and the desire to create spaces that are both beautiful and functional. As we move forward, the industry's commitment to sustainability, technology, and community-building promises a brighter, more efficient, and more connected future for residential living.

Chapter Three: Trenches, Utilities, Hardware, and Footings

"Patience serves as a protection against wrongs as clothes do against cold."

Leonardo da Vinci

Trenching

Trenching is the process of creating narrow excavations in the ground, primarily for the installation of foundations and utilities. It involves marking the excavation area, determining the depth and width based on project requirements, and excavating the soil using equipment like backhoes or trenchers.

Utility Installation

Utility installation in residential construction involves laying out the necessary infrastructure for water, gas, electricity, and sewage. This stage often requires trenching to safely install utility lines below ground level.

Reinforcing Hardware

Reinforcement in construction refers to materials, typically steel, embedded in concrete or masonry structures to enhance strength, load-bearing capacity, and resistance to external forces.

Footing/Foundation Installation

Footings are the structural elements that transfer the load of the house to the ground. They are constructed by digging trenches, placing rebar, and pouring concrete to create a stable base for the foundation.

Construction Site Activities

Construction site activities include site marking, excavating, welding, concreting, brick masonry, and plastering. Effective management of these activities is crucial for project efficiency.

Surveying

Surveying in construction involves creating reference points and markers to guide the construction of new structures. It includes analyzing the site's geography, existing infrastructure, and any subsurface infrastructure.

Trench Mapping

Trench mapping is part of the trenching process and involves documenting the layout and dimensions of trenches to ensure accurate placement of utilities and structural elements.

Site Grading

Site grading adjusts the slope and soil elevation around a construction site. It involves adding or removing soil to create an even surface and ensure a solid foundation for the building.

Concrete Formwork

Concrete formwork is the mold used to hold concrete in place as it hardens. It includes the forms on which concrete is poured and the frames and bracing that provide stability.

Rebar and Hardware Integration

Rebar, or reinforcing bars, are integrated into the concrete to provide tensile strength and improve the structural integrity of the building. This stage involves planning the layout of the rebar and ensuring proper integration with the concrete.

Delivering and Pouring Concrete

This phase involves transporting ready-mix concrete to the construction site and pouring it into the prepared formwork to create the structural elements of the house.

Collaborations with City and County Regulations

Collaboration with local authorities ensures that the construction complies with all relevant building codes and regulations. This includes obtaining necessary permits and inspections throughout the construction process.

Strategic Planning and Execution: The success of residential construction lies in the precision of its foundational work. This chapter delves into the meticulous planning and execution of trenches, utilities, hardware, and footings, which form the bedrock of any structure.

Surveying and Trench Mapping:

- **GPS Technology**: The advent of GPS technology has revolutionized surveying, allowing for rapid and precise outlining of trench locations.
- **Marking Techniques**: Flagged stakes and specialized paint are employed to demarcate plot boundaries and footing positions, ensuring accuracy from the ground up.

Trenching Dynamics:

- **Depth Compliance**: Trenches for utilities and footings are dug to depths sanctioned by local codes and architectural plans.
- **Utility Integration**: Residential lines are connected to municipal infrastructure and are designed to surface just above the final slab level for easy access during subsequent phases.

Soil and Fill Management:

- **Optimal Fill Material**: Selecting and preparing the right fill material is crucial for stability and longevity.
- **Backfilling**: Utility trenches are refilled with excavated soil, while footing trenches remain clear for concrete pouring.

Grading and Formwork:

- **Semi-Finish Grading**: A critical step where the grading crew ensures proper site drainage.
- **Form Setting**: Wooden forms are strategically placed to guide the concrete beyond the soil level, creating a robust base for the structure.

Concrete Footings:

- **Delivery and Pouring**: Concrete with the precise mix for environmental resilience is poured into the trenches, aligning with the wooden forms.
- **Dimensional Standards**: Footings are typically (12") wide by (12") deep for single-story homes, expanding to (15") wide by (18") deep for two-story structures.
- **Garage Foundations**: Include a stem wall that aligns with the interior slab, providing additional support.

Rebar and Hardware Integration:

- **Reinforcement**: Steel reinforcing bars are laid within the footings as per specifications to fortify the concrete.
- **Hardware Installation**: Anchor bolts and connectors are meticulously installed and secured, with bolts embedded a minimum of (7") into the footing and spaced no more than (72") apart, ensuring at least two bolts per foundation piece.

During the concrete pouring process for footings, builders may encounter several common challenges:

1. **Inaccurate Measurements**: Ensuring that trenches are excavated to the correct depth and width is crucial. Using GPS technology and careful surveying can help maintain precision.
2. **Improper Soil Preparation**: The soil must be properly compacted and graded to prevent settling or cracking of the concrete. Adequate site preparation and using the right fill material are key to overcoming this challenge.
3. **Weather Conditions**: Extreme temperatures can affect the curing process of concrete. In cold weather, using heated mixes, accelerants, insulation blankets, and enclosures can help maintain the correct temperature for curing.
4. **Concrete Mix Errors**: The concrete mix must have the correct formulation for the specified strength and environment. Builders should ensure the mix is neither too wet—which can weaken the concrete—nor too dry, which can lead to poor compaction and finishing.
5. **Timing of Pour**: Concrete needs to be poured continuously to avoid cold joints, which can weaken the structure. Coordinating the delivery and having the right equipment on hand is essential to manage this aspect effectively.
6. **Reinforcement Placement**: Incorrect placement of rebar and hardware can compromise the structural integrity. Builders must follow the specifications for rebar placement and ensure that anchor bolts are embedded to the correct depth.

By addressing these challenges with careful planning, precise execution, and the right techniques, builders can ensure a successful concrete pour for footings, setting a strong foundation for the construction project.

Preventing concrete cracks in footings during the curing process is crucial for the structural integrity of a building. Here are some strategies builders can employ:

1. **Proper Soil Preparation**: Ensure the sub-grade is well-compacted and moist before pouring concrete.
2. **Correct Concrete Mix**: Use a low water-cement ratio, ideally not exceeding 0.45, to reduce shrinkage and improve strength.
3. **Controlled Pouring**: Do not add water to ready-mixed concrete during placement, as this can weaken the mixture.
4. **Timely Curing**: Begin curing as soon as finishing is completed. Moisture retention is key, so cover the concrete with wet burlap, plastic sheeting, or use a curing compound to prevent evaporation.
5. **Temperature Management**: Protect the concrete from extreme temperatures using insulating blankets or heaters in cold weather, and by shading and misting the surface in hot weather.
6. **Joint Placement**: Install contraction joints at appropriate intervals to control where cracks occur as the concrete shrinks during curing.

By following these guidelines, builders can significantly reduce the risk of cracking in concrete footings during the curing process.

Here are summaries of case studies that highlight the effectiveness of innovative curing practices in achieving durable and crack-free foundations:

1. **Self-Curing Concrete in High-Rise Buildings**: A study published in the journal Buildings examined the awareness and benefits of self-curing concrete among construction professionals. The research revealed that self-cured concrete, which has the special ability to reduce autogenous shrinkage responsible for early-stage cracking, is particularly beneficial for high-rise buildings and bridges. The study found that self-curing concrete resulted in reduced autogenous shrinkage, crack-free microstructure, and increased durability of the concrete product.
2. **State-of-the-Art Review of Self-Curing Concrete**: Innovative Infrastructure Solutions published a comprehensive review of self-curing concrete, which is designed to cure from the inside out, helping to reduce water waste and eliminate the risk of diminished strength and durability from improper curing. The review discussed various techniques for producing self-curing concrete and the impact of self-curing agents, such as polyethylene glycol and lightweight aggregates. The use of these agents in concrete improves the hydration process, mechanical characteristics, durability, crack susceptibility behavior, and capacity to reduce drying and autogenous shrinkage.

These case studies demonstrate how adopting advanced curing methods can significantly enhance the quality and longevity of concrete foundations, ensuring they remain durable and free of cracks.

Chapter Summary/Key Takeaways

Summary of Chapter Three: Trenches, Utilities, Hardware, and Footings

- **Precision Surveying**: Utilizing GPS technology for accurate trench mapping is essential.
- **Material Selection**: Identifying and properly mixing the appropriate fill material is crucial for foundation stability.
- **Concrete Quality**: Ensuring the concrete delivered is of the exact formulation required for the environment and strength specifications.
- **Trenching**: Adhering to approved depths set by plans and local municipalities for utility and footing trenches.
- **Utility Lines**: Efficiently connecting residential lines to city infrastructure and preparing them for use in the construction phase.
- **Backfilling and Grading**: Backfilling utility line trenches with excavated soil and performing semi-finish grading to ensure proper drainage.
- **Formwork for Concrete**: Setting wood forms to contain the concrete and maintain the correct levels during pouring.
- **Concrete Footings**: Pouring concrete into footing trenches to the specified dimensions, with larger sizes for multi-story homes.
- **Rebar and Hardware Installation**: Placing reinforcing bar and hardware such as hold down anchor bolts and lumber connectors accurately within the footings.

Key Takeaways:

- The chapter emphasizes the importance of accuracy and quality control in the early stages of construction.
- Proper planning and execution of trenches, utilities, and footings are foundational to the durability and safety of the structure.
- Attention to detail in every step, from surveying to concrete pouring, ensures a strong foundation for the residential construction project.

Chapter Four: Sand Layer, Moisture Barrier, Slab Foundation, and Crawlspaces

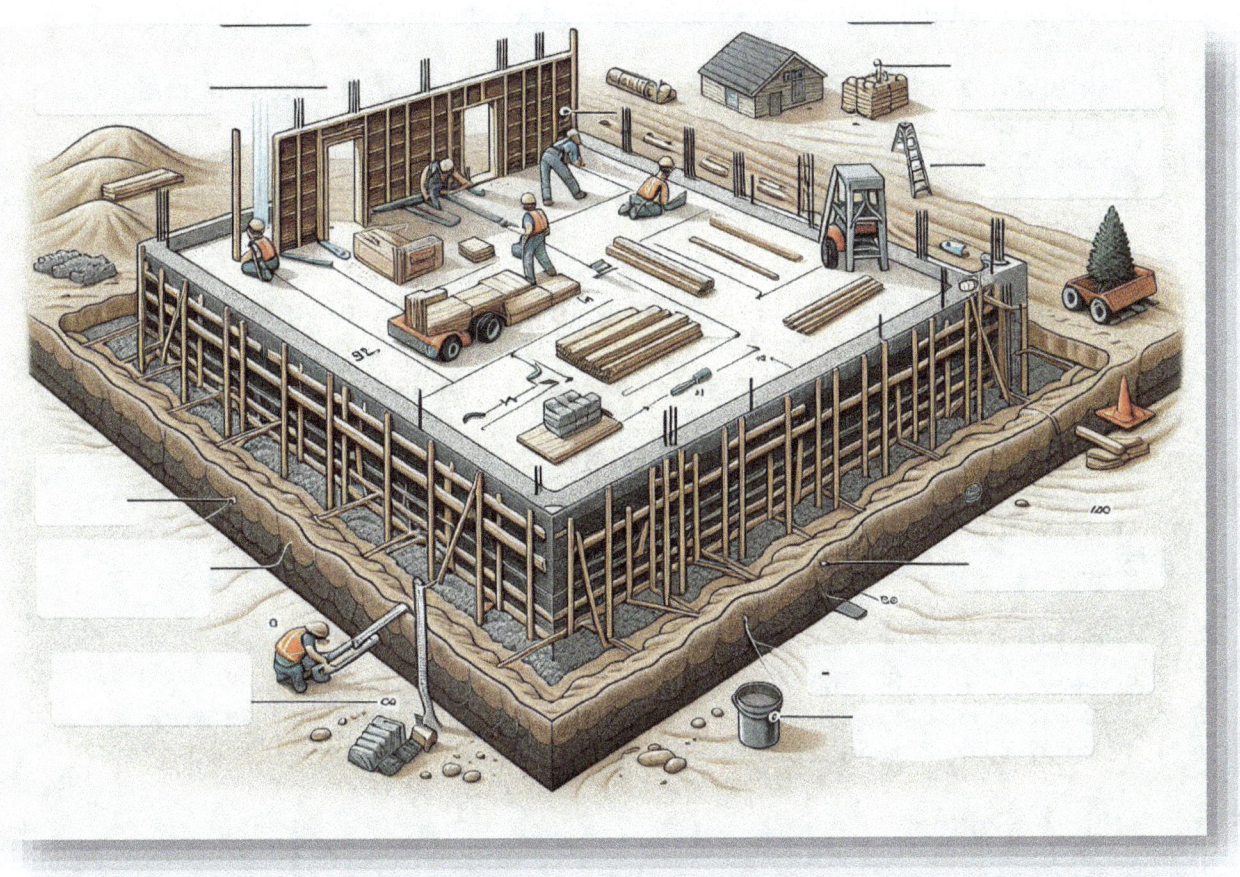

"You can't build a great building on a weak foundation. You must have a solid foundation if you're going to have a strong superstructure."

Gordon B. Hinckley

Sequencing and Installation: The installation of a sand layer or graded gravel layer is the first step in preparing the site for the foundation. This layer provides a stable base for the moisture barrier and concrete footing. The process involves:

1. Site Preparation: Clearing debris and leveling the site.
2. Material Delivery: Transporting sand or gravel to the site.
3. Layering: Spreading the material evenly across the prepared site.
4. Compaction: Compacting the layer to the required density to ensure stability.

Site Activities:

- Excavation of the site to the specified depth.
- Grading the excavated area to create a level base.
- Spreading and compacting the sand or gravel layer.

Moisture Barrier or Ground Cover Installation

Sequencing and Installation: Following the base layer, a moisture barrier is installed to prevent moisture from reaching the foundation. The steps include:

1. Material Selection: Choosing the appropriate moisture barrier material.
2. Placement: Laying the barrier over the sand or gravel layer.
3. Sealing: Ensuring all seams are sealed to prevent moisture penetration.

Site Activities:

- Measuring and cutting the moisture barrier to fit the site dimensions.
- Overlapping and sealing the edges of the barrier.
- Anchoring the barrier to prevent displacement during construction.

Concrete Footing/Foundation Installation

Sequencing and Installation: The concrete footing forms the base of the foundation and is critical for structural integrity. The installation involves:

1. Formwork Setup: Creating the molds for the concrete.
2. Rebar Placement: Installing steel reinforcement within the formwork.
3. Concrete Pouring: Delivering and pouring concrete into the formwork.
4. Curing: Allowing the concrete to set and gain strength.

Site Activities:

- Digging trenches for footings and setting up formwork.
- Installing rebar and safety caps.
- Pouring concrete, ensuring proper compaction, and leveling.

Collaboration with City and County Regulations

Regulatory Compliance: Throughout the construction process, collaboration with city and county regulations is essential to ensure compliance with building codes and standards[7]. This includes:

1. Permit Acquisition: Obtaining necessary permits before construction begins.
2. Inspections: Scheduling regular inspections to verify compliance with codes.
3. Documentation: Maintaining records of all construction activities and approvals.

Site Activities:

- Coordinating with local building officials for inspections.
- Adhering to all building codes and standards during construction.

Making necessary adjustments based on feedback from inspectors.

Critical Preparations:

- **Sand and Moisture Barrier**: Selecting the right type of sand and a robust moisture barrier is essential to protect the slab from ground moisture, which can affect flooring and indoor humidity levels.

Reinforcement Choices:

- **Structural Support**: Depending on the design, the reinforcement may include welded wire mesh, rebar, or tension cables, each providing different levels of strength and flexibility.

Vapor Barrier Installation:

- **Moisture Prevention**: Proper placement of the vapor barrier is crucial to prevent moisture transfer, which can lead to flooring damage and increased humidity within the home.

Construction Steps:

- **Layering Sand**: A 2-inch layer of sand is spread over the native soil for protection, followed by the moisture barrier, and another 2-inch layer of sand.
- **Elevating Mesh**: Precast concrete chairs are used to raise the welded wire mesh 2 inches above the sand surface, ensuring it is properly embedded in the concrete slab.

Concrete Slab Formation:

- **Pouring and Finishing**: The concrete slab is poured over the mesh and carefully finished to prevent undulations. The slab must be at least 4 inches thick for structural integrity.
- **Testing and Compliance**: Workability is assessed with a slump test, and strength is verified by crushing test specimens at set intervals to ensure compliance with ASTM standards.

Post-Tension Concrete:

- **Pre-Stressing Technique**: This method involves placing tendons in a grid pattern within the form, which are then tightened to specified PSI levels after the concrete has partially cured, enhancing strength and span capacity.

Projected Timeline:

- **Approximate Duration**: The entire process, from trenching to the final concrete pour, takes about 2.5 months, laying a solid foundation for the construction project.

MacIntyre/Residential Construction: understanding the Basics.

This chapter emphasizes the importance of meticulous preparation and execution in creating a durable and moisture-resistant slab foundation. By adhering to these detailed steps, builders can ensure a strong and stable base for any residential structure.

Builders can address soil variations and potential settling issues when preparing the sand layer for slab foundations by employing several strategies:

1. **Soil Testing**: Conduct comprehensive soil tests to understand the soil's properties, such as type, moisture content, density, and load-bearing capacity.
2. **Soil Stabilization**: Use stabilization techniques to enhance the soil's load-bearing capabilities. This may involve blending different soil types or adding reinforcing layers like geotextiles.
3. **Proper Grading**: Ensure the site is graded correctly to provide a level base and to facilitate proper drainage away from the foundation.
4. **Compaction**: Compact the soil uniformly to minimize air pockets and create a stable base for the sand layer and foundation.
5. **Moisture Control**: Regulate the moisture content of the soil to achieve optimal compaction and to prevent future settling or expansion.
6. **Quality Sand Layer**: Use a consistent, high-quality sand layer that acts as a cushion and reduces the impact of soil movement on the slab.
7. **Vapor Barrier**: Install a robust vapor barrier over the sand layer to prevent moisture transfer from the ground into the slab, which can affect the foundation over time.

By following these steps, builders can effectively manage soil variations and mitigate settling risks, ensuring a durable and stable foundation for the construction project.

Builders should be vigilant for several common signs of soil settlement during and after construction, which can indicate potential issues with the foundation:

1. **Cracks in Drywall**: Large cracks in drywall that aren't due to normal settling may signal a more serious problem.
2. **Misaligned Doors and Windows**: If doors and windows become difficult to open or close, it could be due to shifting of the foundation.
3. **Large Cracks in Concrete Slab**: Visible cracks in the concrete slab, basement floors, or other foundational elements are often signs of settlement.
4. **Gaps Between Ceiling and Walls**: Any separation between the ceiling and walls can be a result of the house settling.
5. **Uneven or Sloped Floorboards**: Noticeable sloping or unevenness in the flooring can indicate that the foundation is settling.

These signs can help builders identify potential settlement issues early on, allowing for timely interventions to prevent further damage. It's important to address these signs promptly to maintain the structural integrity of the building.

Here are some examples of real-world projects where proactive measures effectively prevented significant damage due to soil settlement:

1. **Machine Learning in Finland**: A study focused on optimizing soil settlement and consolidation prediction in Finland's clays using machine-learning regressions with Bayesian hyperparameter selection. This approach allowed for accurate predictions of pre-consolidation stress, enabling engineers to take preventive measures against soil settlement, thus ensuring the stability and durability of structures built on these clays.
2. **Trenching Projects**: An article discussed best practices for soil settlement management in trenching projects. By conducting thorough soil investigations before construction and implementing ground improvement techniques such as compaction and soil stabilization, builders were able to minimize soil settlement. This proactive approach ensured structural safety, worker safety, and project success.
3. **Intermediate Soil State Management**: Research investigated the relationship between the state of intermediate soil and settlement control measures in new tunnel projects under existing stations. By understanding this relationship, engineers were able to implement settlement control measures effectively, preventing damage to the existing station structures during the construction of new tunnels.

These examples demonstrate the importance of proactive planning and the use of innovative techniques to address soil settlement issues, ensuring the longevity and safety of construction projects.

Crawl Spaces - The Underlying Details

Introduction

Crawl spaces are an integral part of residential construction, providing access to plumbing, electrical systems, and more. This chapter outlines the sequence of subcontractor trades and essential considerations for constructing a functional and code-compliant crawl space.

Sequencing of Subcontractor Trades

The construction of a crawl space is a coordinated effort that involves various trades. Here's the recommended sequence:

1. **Grading Contractor**: Begins with site preparation, ensuring proper elevation and grading for drainage.
2. **Ground Preparation**: Involves compacting the soil and preparing the base for the crawl space.
3. **Plumbing**: Plumbers install the necessary piping and infrastructure before the concrete is poured.
4. **Concrete**: The concrete contractor pours the footing and, if applicable, a rat slab for the crawl space floor.
5. **Electrical**: Electricians run conduit and wiring necessary for lighting and other electrical needs in the crawl space.

6. **Ground Cover (Vapor Barrier)**: A thick polyethylene sheet is laid across the ground to prevent moisture from rising into the crawl space.
7. **Radon Mitigation System**: If required, a radon mitigation system is installed to vent radon gas out of the crawl space.
8. **Site Drainage**: Ensuring proper drainage around and under the crawl space is critical to prevent water accumulation.
9. **Code Required Ventilation**: Ventilation is installed according to local building codes to manage moisture and air quality.
10. **Code Required Access and Headroom**: Finally, access points are created with the required headroom for easy entry and maintenance.

Considerations for Crawl Space Construction

Ground Cover and Moisture Control

- **Vapor Barrier**: A minimum of 6-mil polyethylene sheeting should cover the entire crawl space ground to prevent moisture intrusion.
- **Sealing**: All seams must be overlapped by 12 inches and sealed with tape designed for this purpose.

Radon Mitigation

- **Testing**: Conduct radon testing to determine if a mitigation system is necessary.
- **Installation**: Install a radon mitigation system that includes a vent pipe and fan to reduce radon levels.

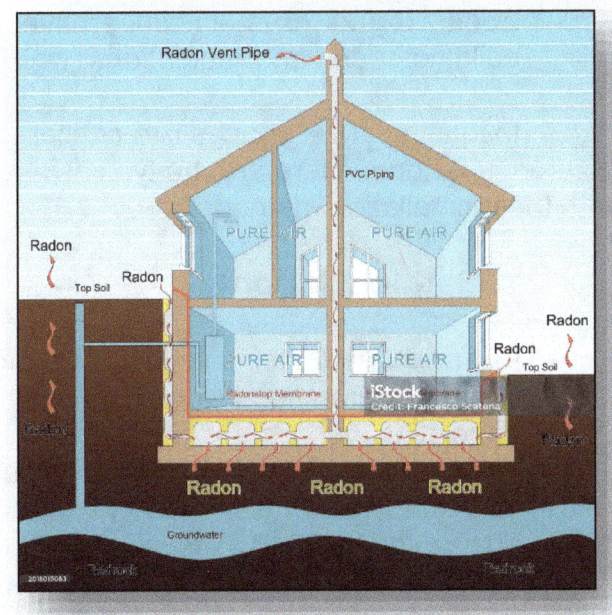

Ventilation

- **Vent Placement**: Vents should be placed to allow for cross-ventilation, with one square foot of vent area for every 150 square feet of crawl space.
- **Vent Wells**: Install vent wells to prevent soil and debris from blocking the vents.

Access and Headroom

- **Access Size**: The minimum size for an access opening is 18 inches by 24 inches.
- **Location**: Place access in a location that does not require the removal of obstacles or the use of portable ladders for entry.

- **Headroom**: Provide adequate headroom within the crawl space for maintenance and repair work.

Site Drainage

- **Slope**: The ground should slope away from the foundation to prevent water pooling.
- **Drainage Systems**: Consider installing French drains or other systems to manage excess water effectively.

Other Considerations

- **Insulation**: We will discuss the types of insulation suitable for crawl spaces and the methods for proper installation to maintain energy efficiency below.
- **Pest Control**: During the design and construction phases it is critical to address and provide measures to prevent pests such as rodents or insects from entering and inhabiting the crawl space.
- **Structural Support**: It is extremely important to ensure that the construction team is inspecting and maintaining the structural supports within the crawl space, such as piers and beams during trade coordination within the crawlspace.
- **Local Regulations**: It is imperative that all subtrades comply with local building codes and regulations, which can vary significantly by region.

Insulating crawl spaces is a critical step in ensuring energy efficiency and comfort in a home. Here are the typical insulation options for crawl spaces, along with their installation methods:

1. Batt Insulation

- **Description**: Batt insulation, also known as blanket insulation, is made of fiberglass or mineral wool. It's a cost-effective option that comes in pre-cut panels.
- **Installation**: It's typically installed between floor joists in the crawl space. Vapor barriers may be used to protect against moisture, and it's essential to ensure the insulation fits snugly without gaps.

2. Spray Foam Insulation

- **Description**: Spray foam insulation provides an air seal and thermal barrier. It's available in open-cell and closed-cell varieties, with closed-cell providing a higher R-value and moisture resistance.
- **Installation**: Professional installation is recommended as it involves spraying the foam directly onto the crawl space surfaces, creating a continuous barrier that conforms to irregular shapes and provides excellent air sealing.

3. Rigid Foam Insulation

- **Description**: Rigid foam insulation, such as extruded polystyrene (XPS) or polyisocyanurate, is durable and moisture-resistant. It comes in rigid panels that can be cut to fit.
- **Installation**: Rigid foam is installed against crawl space walls or the underside of the floor above. Panels must be securely attached and seams sealed with tape or spray foam to prevent air leakage.

4. Cellulose Insulation

- **Description**: Cellulose insulation is made from recycled paper products and is treated with fire retardants. It's an eco-friendly option that can be blown into spaces.
- **Installation**: This type of insulation is typically blown into place, filling gaps, and providing a dense, effective barrier. It's important to ensure that the crawl space is dry as cellulose can absorb moisture.

Considerations for Installation:

- **Moisture Control**: Regardless of the insulation type, controlling moisture with a vapor barrier is crucial to prevent mold and structural damage.
- **Ventilation**: Adequate ventilation must be maintained to manage moisture levels, especially in vented crawl spaces.
- **Sealing**: All insulation should be properly sealed to prevent air infiltration, which can significantly reduce its effectiveness.
- **Code Compliance**: Ensure that all materials and installation methods comply with local building codes and regulations.

Conclusion

A well-designed crawl space is vital for the longevity and integrity of a home. By following the proper sequence of subcontractor trades and adhering to building codes, you can ensure a safe and efficient crawl space that stands the test of time.

Chapter Summary/Key Takeaways

Summary of Chapter Four: Sand Layer, Moisture Barrier, and Slab Foundation

- **Sand and Moisture Barrier**: The selection and distribution of sand and a ground moisture barrier are critical for protecting the slab from moisture.
- **Reinforcement Options**: The slab may be reinforced with welded-wire-mesh, rebar, or tension cables, depending on the specified system.
- **Vapor Barrier Placement**: Correct installation of the vapor barrier is essential to prevent future moisture transfer, which can affect flooring and indoor humidity.

- **Sand Layering**: A 2-inch sand layer is placed over native soil, followed by a moisture barrier and another 2-inch sand layer, ensuring a total of 4 inches between the sand top and footing.
- **Concrete Reinforcement**: Precast concrete chairs elevate the welded wire mesh for proper embedment into the concrete slab.
- **Concrete Slab Pouring**: The concrete slab is poured to a minimum thickness of 4 inches and finished to prevent undulations.
- **Concrete Quality**: The concrete's strength and workability are tested to comply with ASTM standards.
- **Post-Tension Concrete**: This method pre-stresses the concrete to enable higher strength and longer spans, countering concrete's lower tensile strength.

Key Takeaways:

- Proper preparation and layering of materials beneath the slab foundation are vital for long-term durability.
- Adherence to building codes and standards during the concrete pouring and curing processes ensures structural integrity.
- Innovative techniques like post-tensioning enhance the foundation's ability to support greater loads and span wider areas.

These points highlight the importance of meticulous planning and execution in laying a strong and stable foundation for residential construction projects.

MacIntyre/Residential Construction: understanding the Basics.

Chapter Five: General Framing

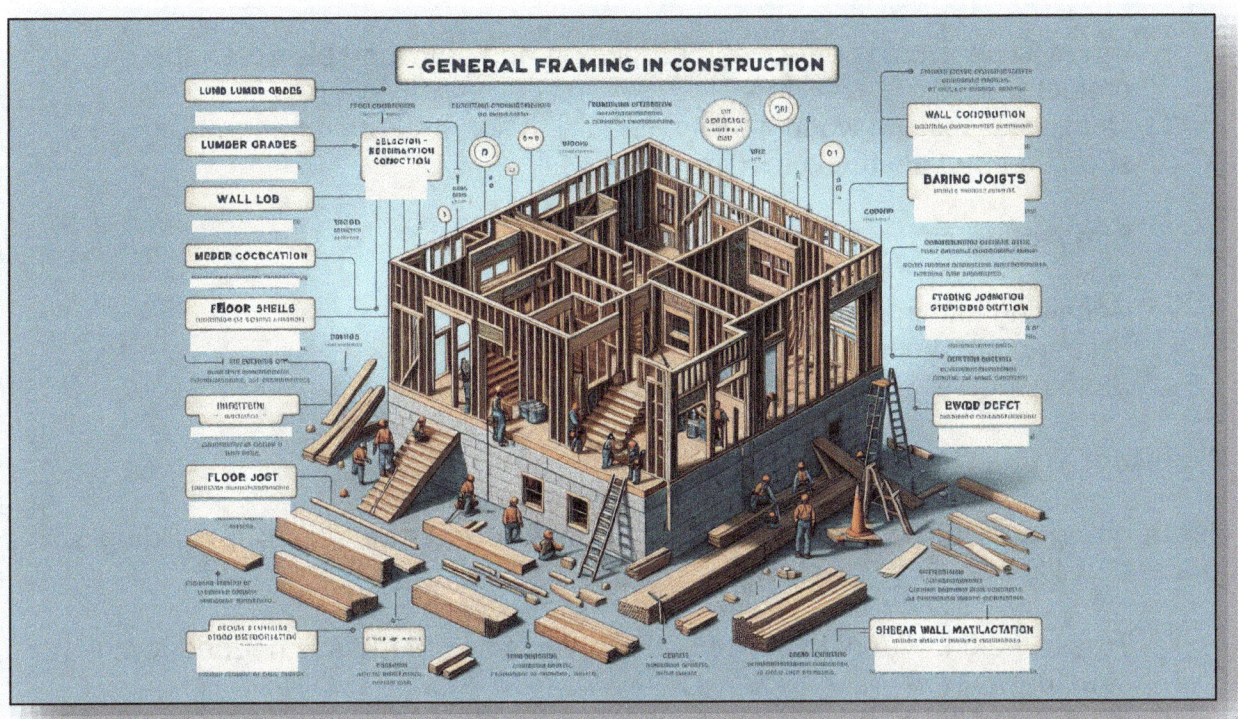

"A rising tide doesn't raise people who don't have a boat. We have to build the boat for them. We have to give them the basic infrastructure to rise with the tide."

    Rahul Gandhi

Structural Engineered/Designed Framing Systems

    Sequencing and Installation: Structural engineered framing systems, also known as advanced framing or optimum value engineering (OVE), optimize material usage and increase energy efficiency. The process typically involves:

1. Design Planning: Creating detailed architectural drawings and selecting appropriate framing systems.
2. Material Selection: Choosing high-grade materials for durability and compliance with design requirements.
3. Assembly: Cutting, shaping, and assembling components into the specified design.

    Site Activities:

- Setting up formwork for concrete foundations.
- Installing steel reinforcement and pouring concrete.
- Erecting the structural frame and ensuring proper alignment.

Lumber Selection

MacIntyre/Residential Construction: understanding the Basics.

Sequencing and Installation: Selecting the right lumber is crucial for the integrity of the construction. Factors to consider include:

1. Wood Type: Deciding between hardwood and softwood based on the project's needs.
2. Quality: Assessing wood density, texture, color, and grain pattern for structural and aesthetic requirements.

Site Activities:

- Receiving and inspecting lumber deliveries.
- Preparing and cutting lumber to specifications.
- Storing lumber properly to prevent damage.

Wall/Roof Truss Construction and Installation

Sequencing and Installation: Wall and roof trusses form the core of a building's roof and walls. The stages include:

1. Truss Design: Planning the type and dimensions of trusses needed for the structure.
2. Manufacturing: Fabricating trusses in a controlled environment to ensure precision.
3. Installation: Transporting and securing trusses to the building's frame.

Site Activities:

- Preparing the site for truss delivery.
- Using cranes to lift and place trusses.

Collaboration with City and County Regulations

Regulatory Compliance: Adhering to local regulations is vital for legal and safety reasons. This includes:

1. Permit Acquisition: Securing permits for construction, electrical work, plumbing, etc.
2. Inspections: Arranging inspections at various stages to ensure code compliance.
3. Documentation: Keeping detailed records of all construction activities and regulatory approvals.

Site Activities:

- Meeting with inspectors and addressing any issues.
- Ensuring all construction practices meet local codes and standards.

    Adjusting plans as needed to comply with regulatory feedback.

Selecting the Right Lumber Grade

- The lumber grade is critical where wood interfaces with concrete, ensuring durability and structural integrity.

MEP Component Placement

- This construction phase involves the strategic placement of rough Mechanical, Electrical, and Plumbing (MEP) components.

Coordinating Crews and Equipment

- Effective coordination is essential among Framers, Plumbers, and Electricians to manage space and workflow efficiently.

Construction Activities

Wall Construction

- Walls are constructed on the slab and then raised into position.
- Headers are installed above openings in wall sections to facilitate load transfer, with sizes determined by the span and specified by the designer.

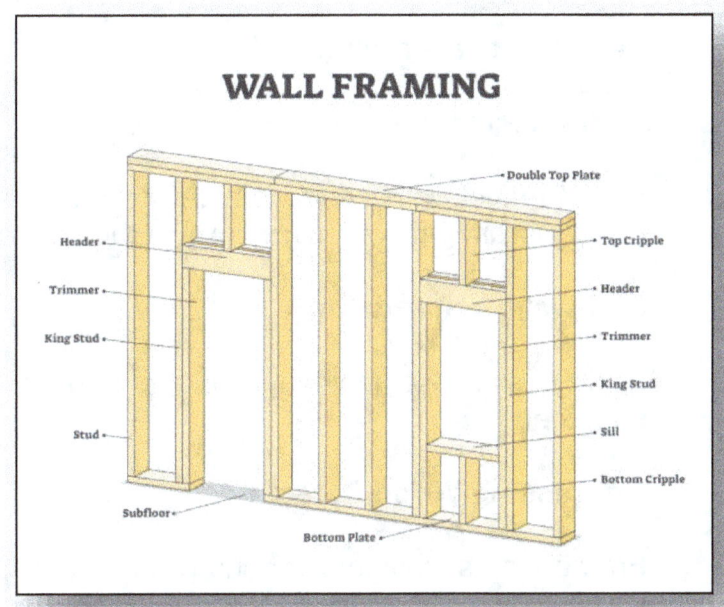

Bearing Walls

- Bearing walls feature a single wood sill plate, vertical studs spaced at 16" on center, and dual top plates for added stability.

Non-Bearing Walls

- Constructed with a wider stud spacing of 24" on center, these walls are secured to the slab using shot pins and include blocking for drywall support.

First Level Framing

Foundation Interaction

- Framing begins once the concrete achieves sufficient compressive strength, with precautions taken to prevent wood and concrete conflict.

Wall Positioning

- Walls are erected over anchor bolts extending from the footings, with all necessary hardware installed and secured.

Floor Joists and Sheathing

Joist Installation

- I joists are installed over the first level's top plates, with solid joists at specified locations and rim joists along the perimeter.

Subfloor Installation

- A plywood subfloor is laid once joists are in place, providing a stable base for subsequent construction.

Second Level Framing

Wall Assembly

- Second-level walls are assembled on the subfloor platform and secured with nails, mirroring the specifications of the first level.

Stairway Construction

- During this phase, stairway stringers and landings are also framed and sheathed.

Addressing Wood Defects

- Framers must navigate various wood defects, such as bowing, cupping, and knots, which can affect material quality and installation.

Shear Wall & Hardware Installation

Enhancing Structural Integrity with Shear Walls

- Once the utility lines are nearing completion, the installation of OSB or plywood shear walls begins. These walls are crucial for reinforcing the structure against lateral forces such as wind or seismic activity.
- The placement of shear walls is a strategic decision made by the structural engineer to optimize the building's strength.

Securing the Framework

- Structural straps and hardware components are meticulously attached to the framing members, following the precise specifications laid out by the design team.

Roof Trusses Installation

Efficient Truss Assembly

- With the wall framing complete, pre-engineered wood trusses are delivered and carefully lifted into place.
- A designated area near the HVAC unit is left open to ensure easy access for installation, followed by the placement of a plywood mechanical platform.

Securing and Fire Blocking

- The trusses are firmly secured using a combination of nails and framing clips. Fire blocking is strategically placed at the ridge and eaves to prevent the spread of fire within concealed spaces.

Metal Ties for Added Security

- Roof trusses are further anchored to the structure using a variety of metal ties, including Simpson Strong Tie models H8, H2.5, MTS12, and H10, ensuring robust attachment.

Fascia, Trim Boards, and Sheathing

Final Touches to the Roof Structure

- Outriggers are installed at the roof's apex or open rake sides to support the fascia board, which is then meticulously installed.
- The starter board, often consisting of shiplap, is added around the eave perimeter for both structural purposes and visual appeal.
- OSB sheathing is laid across the trusses to form a solid roof deck, with H Clips at panel joints and 1/8" gaps between panels to accommodate thermal movement.

Thermal expansion and contraction of materials

Thermal expansion and contraction are physical processes that occur when a material changes in volume in response to temperature changes. When a material is heated, its particles gain energy and move more vigorously, causing the material to expand. Conversely, when the material cools down, the particles lose energy and move less, resulting in the material contracting. These phenomena are important considerations in construction and manufacturing, as they can affect the integrity and performance of materials and structures. For example, gaps are left between panels in roof sheathing to allow for the expansion and contraction of the material, preventing potential damage or warping.

Not accounting for thermal movement in construction can lead to several practical issues:

- **Structural Damage**: Without space for expansion and contraction, materials can warp, crack, or break due to the stress caused by temperature changes.
- **Safety Hazards**: Compromised structural elements can pose safety risks to occupants and passersby.
- **Increased Maintenance Costs**: Frequent repairs and maintenance may be required to address damage caused by thermal movement.
- **Operational Disruptions**: In cases like bridges, improper thermal movement accommodation can lead to closures and traffic disruptions for repair work.
- **Reduced Lifespan**: The longevity of the structure can be significantly reduced due to the ongoing stress and damage.

These implications highlight the importance of incorporating design elements such as expansion joints and flexible materials to allow for thermal movement in structures.

Here are some examples of structures that are well-designed to accommodate thermal movement:

- **Bridges**: Many bridges are equipped with expansion joints that allow for the natural expansion and contraction of materials due to temperature changes. This prevents structural damage and maintains the integrity of the bridge.
- **Sidewalks**: Concrete sidewalks often have small gaps between sections, known as expansion joints, which allow for thermal movement. Without these joints, sidewalks could crack and buckle with temperature fluctuations.
- **Buildings**: Modern buildings, especially those with large surface areas like skyscrapers, incorporate design elements such as curtain walls that have the ability to move slightly to accommodate thermal expansion and contraction.
- **Piping Systems**: Industrial piping systems use flexible couplings and expansion joints to manage thermal movement, ensuring that pipes do not rupture or leak due to temperature changes.

These examples demonstrate the importance of considering thermal movement in the design and construction of various structures to ensure their longevity and safety.

Historically, there have been several instances where structures have failed due to inadequate consideration for temperature effects:

- **Tacoma Narrows Bridge (1940)**: Known as "Galloping Gertie," this bridge in Washington State collapsed due to aeroelastic flutter caused by wind. While not directly related to thermal expansion, the failure highlighted the importance of considering environmental factors in engineering.

- **Quebec Bridge (1907)**: The bridge collapsed during construction, and while the primary cause was attributed to design flaws and overloading, the temperature variations and thermal expansion were also contributing factors to the stresses that led to the failure.
- **Hyatt Regency Walkway Collapse (1981)**: In Kansas City, the walkways collapsed due to a design flaw in the connections, but the temperature variations within the atrium could have contributed to the material fatigue over time.

These examples underscore the critical need for engineers to account for temperature effects and other environmental conditions when designing structures.

Chapter Summary/Key Takeaways

Summary: Chapter Five delves into the essential aspects of framing in construction, emphasizing the selection of appropriate lumber grades, the strategic placement of MEP components, and the importance of coordinating various crews and equipment. It details the construction activities involved in wall construction, the installation of floor joists and sheathing, and the assembly of second-level framing. The chapter also addresses the challenges posed by wood defects and the role of shear walls in enhancing structural integrity.

Key Takeaways:

1. **Lumber Grade Selection**: The choice of lumber grade is crucial for areas where wood meets concrete, affecting the structure's durability and integrity.
2. **MEP Component Placement**: The careful placement of Mechanical, Electrical, and Plumbing components during framing is vital for the building's functionality.
3. **Crew Coordination**: Efficient management of space and workflow among framers, plumbers, and electricians is essential for a smooth construction process.
4. **Wall Construction**: Walls are built on the slab and then raised into position, with headers installed above openings to support load transfer.
5. **Bearing and Non-Bearing Walls**: Bearing walls have specific structural features for stability, while non-bearing walls have different requirements for stud spacing and attachment.
6. **Foundation Interaction**: Framing starts after the concrete reaches adequate strength, with measures taken to prevent adverse interactions between wood and concrete.
7. **Floor Joists and Sheathing**: The installation of I joists and the laying of a plywood subfloor form the basis for the next construction stages.
8. **Second-Level Framing**: The second-level walls are constructed with the same precision as the first level, ensuring consistency and strength.

9. **Stairway Construction**: The framing and sheathing of stairway stringers and landings are integral to the building's structure.
10. **Wood Defects Management**: Framers must address various wood defects to ensure material quality and proper installation.
11. **Shear Wall Installation**: Shear walls are installed to support lateral loads and improve the building's overall structural integrity.

This chapter provides a comprehensive guide to the general framing process, highlighting the importance of each step and consideration in ensuring a structurally sound and durable building.

Chapter Six: Mechanical, Electrical, and Plumbing (MEP)

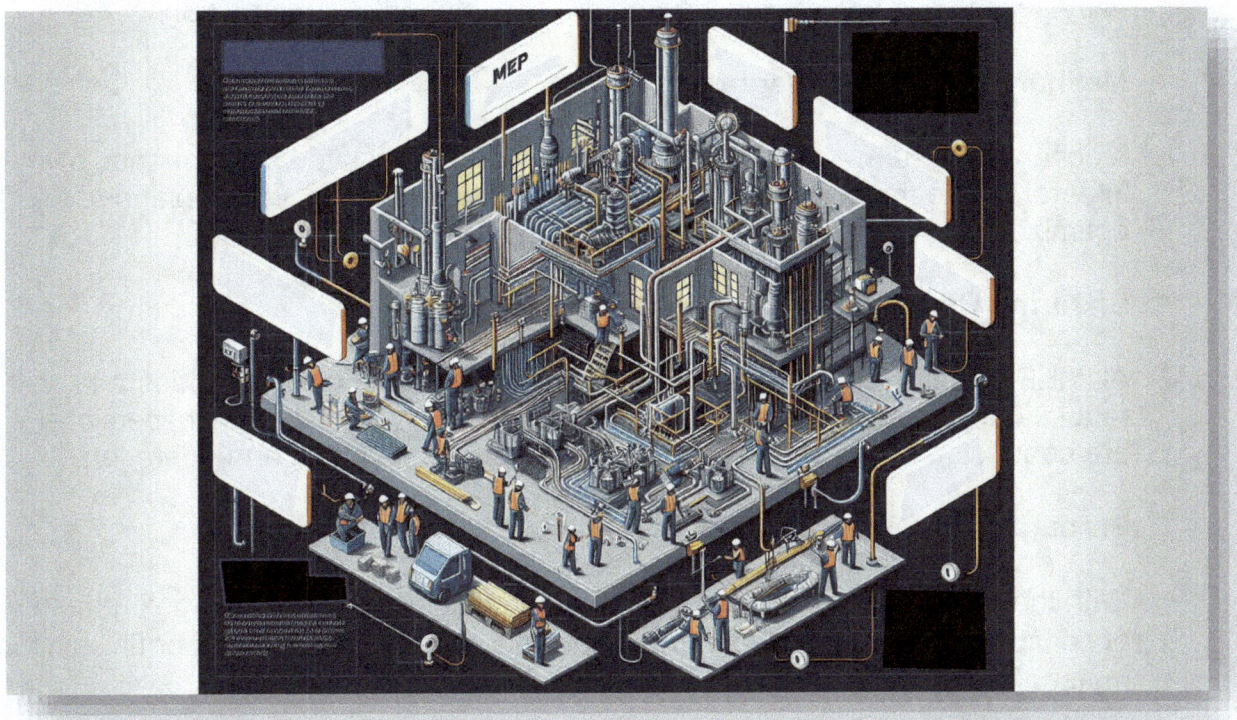

"Systems thinking is a discipline for seeing wholes. It is a framework for seeing interrelationships rather than things, for seeing 'patterns of change' rather than 'static snapshots."

Peter Senge

Coordinated Installation of MEP Lines

- As the second-level walls are framed, a coordinated effort among electricians, plumbers, and mechanical technicians is crucial for the installation of supply lines. This is strategically done before the application of exterior sheathing and interior drywall to ensure unobstructed access through the open framework.

Electrical System Setup

- Electrical lines are meticulously routed and securely terminated in designated junction boxes. This setup prepares the electrical system for future connections and ensures compliance with safety standards.

Plumbing System Configuration

- Plumbing supply lines and vent pipes are installed with precision, extending beyond the surface where the walls and roof will be finished. This allows for easy access and adjustments during the final stages of construction.

Mechanical System Integration

- Mechanical systems, including HVAC ductwork and related components, are integrated into the building's structure. The placement is carefully planned to optimize performance and maintain aesthetic appeal.

Ensuring Compliance and Safety

- All MEP installations are performed in accordance with building codes and regulations to ensure the safety and functionality of the systems. Inspections are conducted at various stages to verify proper installation and operation.

Preparing for Finishing Work

- With the MEP systems in place, the structure is now ready for the next phase of construction, which includes the application of exterior and interior finishing materials.

Inspections

Inspectors verify compliance during MEP installations through a series of steps:

1. **Review of Design Documents**: Inspectors examine the MEP design plans to ensure they meet the relevant codes and standards.
2. **On-Site Inspections**: They conduct on-site visits to observe the installation process, ensuring that it aligns with the approved plans.
3. **Testing and Commissioning**: Inspectors witness testing and commissioning activities to confirm that the systems function as intended.
4. **Ensuring Code Adherence**: They check for adherence to local, state, and national regulations, such as the International Building Code (IBC) and National Electrical Code (NEC).
5. **Quality Assurance**: Regular quality control checks are performed to verify that the MEP systems are installed correctly and in compliance with the design intent.
6. **Documentation**: Inspectors review all documentation and certifications related to the MEP systems to ensure everything is in order.
7. **Final Approval**: Once all inspections and tests are satisfactory, inspectors provide the final sign-off, indicating that the MEP systems are compliant and ready for use.

These steps help ensure that MEP installations are safe, functional, and efficient, adhering to the required building codes and standards.

Challenges

During HVAC ductwork installation, several challenges may arise, including:

- **Sizing the HVAC System**: Properly sizing the system to match the building's layout is crucial. An undersized system won't maintain a comfortable temperature, and an oversized system can waste energy.
- **Ductwork Design and Installation**: Poor ductwork design or installation can lead to air leaks, uneven airflow, and reduced energy efficiency. It's important to follow best practices and guidelines for ductwork design and installation.
- **Electrical and Control Wiring**: Complexities in electrical and control wiring can cause poor system performance or even failure. Proper training and certification are essential for HVAC contractors.
- **Limited Access Spaces**: Installing ductwork in tight or hard-to-reach areas can be challenging and may require specialized equipment.
- **Precise Alignment**: Accurate alignment of duct sections is crucial for optimal airflow and system performance but can be time-consuming.

These challenges highlight the importance of careful planning, precise execution, and adherence to industry standards during HVAC ductwork installation.

During plumbing installation, professionals may encounter several challenges:

- **Clogged Drains and Pipes**: Blockages caused by grease, hair, and foreign objects are common issues that can disrupt the plumbing system.
- **Leaky Faucets and Pipes**: Leaks can lead to water wastage and potential structural damage if not addressed promptly.
- **Water Heater Problems**: Issues such as inadequate hot water supply, strange noises, or system failures require immediate attention.
- **Complex Layouts**: In commercial construction, plumbing design must navigate complex layouts and ensure compliance with codes and regulations.
- **Material Selection**: Choosing the right materials for durability and compatibility with existing systems is crucial.
- **Waste Management**: Properly designing systems for waste and sewage disposal is essential for environmental and health safety.
- **Coordination with Other Trades**: Plumbing must be coordinated with other construction activities to ensure seamless integration.
- **Limited Access**: In some buildings, especially commercial ones, access to plumbing systems can be restricted, making repairs and installations more challenging.
- **Water Pressure Issues**: Ensuring consistent water pressure throughout the system can be a recurring challenge.

These challenges highlight the need for careful planning, skilled workmanship, and adherence to safety standards in plumbing installation.

During electrical installation, professionals may encounter several challenges:

- **Faulty Wiring**: Incorrectly installed wiring can lead to power outages, circuit overloads, and even fires. Ensuring proper installation techniques and adherence to safety standards is crucial.
- **Outdated Electrical Panels**: Older electrical panels may not support the energy demands of modern appliances and can be a safety hazard. Upgrading to current standards is often necessary.
- **Overloaded Circuits**: Circuits that carry more current than they are rated for can overheat and cause fires. Proper load distribution and circuit design are essential to prevent overloading.
- **Space Constraints**: In new builds, limited space and accessibility can make it difficult to route wires effectively and maintain proper cable management.
- **Compliance with Codes and Regulations**: Electricians must be familiar with and adhere to local building codes and electrical regulations to ensure safety and legality.
- **Integration of New Technologies**: Incorporating smart home systems, automation, and renewable energy sources requires careful planning and execution.
- **Energy Efficiency**: Implementing energy-saving solutions and optimizing power distribution are important for reducing environmental impact and operational costs.

These challenges highlight the importance of careful planning, skilled workmanship, and adherence to safety standards in electrical installation.

Chapter Summary/Key Takeaways

This chapter outlines the critical coordination and installation of MEP systems in construction. It emphasizes the importance of integrating these systems early in the framing stage to ensure easy access and efficient workflow. The chapter covers the meticulous routing of electrical lines, the precise installation of plumbing systems, and the careful integration of mechanical systems, including HVAC ductwork. It also highlights the necessity of adhering to building codes and safety regulations throughout the installation process.

Key Takeaways:

1. **Coordinated Effort**: A synchronized approach among electricians, plumbers, and mechanical technicians is essential for the timely and efficient installation of MEP systems.
2. **Strategic Installation**: MEP lines are installed before exterior sheathing and interior drywall to provide unobstructed access through the framework.
3. **Electrical System Setup**: Electrical lines are carefully routed and terminated in junction boxes, preparing for future connections, and ensuring safety compliance.

4. **Plumbing System Configuration**: Plumbing lines and vent pipes are installed to extend beyond the finished surfaces, allowing for easy access during later construction stages.
5. **Mechanical System Integration**: HVAC ductwork and components are integrated into the building's structure with a focus on optimizing performance and maintaining design aesthetics.
6. **Compliance and Safety**: All installations comply with building codes and regulations, with inspections verifying proper installation and operation.
7. **Preparation for Finishing Work**: With MEP systems in place, the structure is ready for the next construction phase, including the application of finishing materials.
8. **Challenges in HVAC Installation**: Proper system sizing, ductwork design, electrical wiring, access to tight spaces, and precise alignment are all challenges that must be managed to ensure optimal system performance.

By following the guidelines and considerations presented in this chapter, construction professionals can ensure that MEP systems are installed effectively, safely, and in compliance with all necessary standards.

Chapter Seven: Exterior Flashing and Waterproofing

"The first rule of sustainability is to align with natural forces, or at least not try to defy them."

Paul Hawken

Waterproofing is a critical aspect of construction that protects buildings from water ingress, which can cause significant damage over time. Understanding the strategic considerations and refined construction activities for effective waterproofing is essential for any construction project.

Identifying Critical Junctions and Transitions The first step in effective waterproofing is identifying critical junctions and transitions in the building's design. These are potential weak points where water can enter, such as where different materials meet or where the roof connects to the walls. By pinpointing these areas early on, you can plan for additional protection to prevent water ingress.

Selection of Flashing Components Choosing the right flashing components is crucial for effective waterproofing. Rigid metal and flexible sheet membranes are commonly used, but their selection should be based on the specific needs of each junction. Factors like exposure to the elements, thermal movement, and the angle of water contact will influence which materials are best suited for the job.

Integration with the Weather Resistant Barrier (WRB) A Weather Resistant Barrier (WRB) is a sheet or coating that resists water but allows water vapor to pass through, preventing moisture buildup within the walls. Integrating flashing components with the WRB must be meticulously planned to ensure a seamless barrier against moisture. This includes overlapping and sealing all layers to prevent any potential leaks.

Roof and Wall Flashings Roof and wall flashings should be designed to work in tandem, providing comprehensive protection against water. These flashings direct water away from the building and are especially important around openings like windows and doors. Ensuring that these components work together effectively will enhance the building's waterproofing system.

Chemical Compatibility The chemical compatibility of all materials used in the waterproofing process is essential to prevent degradation and ensure longevity. Incompatible materials can react with each other, leading to premature failure of the waterproofing system. Always check the manufacturer's specifications to ensure that all materials used are compatible.

Refined Construction Activities for Window Flashing & WRB Window flashings must be applied with precision and fully integrated with the WRB. This requires following detailed guidelines provided by the designer or manufacturer. Installation principles such as maintaining WRB continuity, sealing for air leakage, ensuring proper alignment, and facilitating water drainage are fundamental to every method. Adherence to industry standards like AAMA 2400 and ASTM e2112-07 is crucial, with deviations addressed through Requests for Information (RFI) to the design team for clarification.

Advanced Flashing Techniques Advanced flashing techniques can further bolster the waterproofing system. This includes the use of multi-part sill pans, through-wall flashings, and corner reinforcements. Swing door flashing follows similar principles, with an emphasis on shingle lapping, corner reinforcement, and the use of compatible sealants.

Installation Locations for Optimal Protection Metal and flexible flashings are strategically installed at deck and roof junctions, transitions between dissimilar materials, wall penetrations, building corners, and around windows, doors, and railing connections. This process requires the coordinated efforts of window installers, framers, siders, roofers, and sheet metal subcontractors to achieve a watertight exterior.

Strategic Considerations for Effective Waterproofing:

- Identifying critical junctions and transitions is paramount for preventing water ingress.
- Selection of flashing components, such as rigid metal and flexible sheet membranes, should be based on the specific needs of each junction.
- Integration with the Weather Resistant Barrier (WRB) must be meticulously planned to ensure a seamless barrier against moisture.

MacIntyre/Residential Construction: understanding the Basics.

- Roof and wall flashings should be designed to work in tandem, providing comprehensive protection.
- Chemical compatibility of all materials is essential to prevent degradation and ensure longevity.

Refined Construction Activities for Window Flashing & WRB:

- Window flashings must be applied with precision and fully integrated with the WRB, following detailed guidelines provided by the designer or manufacturer.
- Installation principles such as maintaining WRB continuity, sealing for air leakage, ensuring proper alignment, and facilitating water drainage are fundamental to every method.
- Adherence to industry standards like AAMA 2400 and ASTM e2112-07 is crucial, with deviations addressed through Requests for Information (RFI) to the design team for clarification.
- Dupont Tyvek is recognized for its comprehensive window installation details, which serve as a valuable reference.

Advanced Flashing Techniques:

- All flashing components should be integrated in a shingle fashion to ensure proper water shedding.
- Advanced techniques include the use of multi-part sill pans, through-wall flashings, and corner reinforcements to bolster the waterproofing system.
- Swing door flashing follows similar principles, with an emphasis on shingle lapping, corner reinforcement, and the use of compatible sealants.

Installation Locations for Optimal Protection:

- Metal and flexible flashings are strategically installed at deck and roof junctions, transitions between dissimilar materials, wall penetrations, building corners, and around windows, doors, and railing connections.
- This process requires the coordinated efforts of window installers, framers, siders, roofers, and sheet metal subcontractors to achieve a watertight exterior.

This enhanced chapter provides a comprehensive guide to exterior flashing and waterproofing, emphasizing the importance of strategic planning, material selection, and meticulous installation practices to safeguard buildings against water damage.

Contractors ensure proper integration between the Weather Resistant Barrier (WRB) and metal flashings at deck junctions through a meticulous, multi-step process:

1. **Identify Critical Junctions**: First, they identify where the WRB and metal flashings will intersect with the deck junctions.

2. **Select Appropriate Materials**: They choose compatible materials for the WRB and metal flashings to ensure chemical compatibility and long-term durability.
3. **Install in Shingle Fashion**: The metal flashing is installed in a shingle fashion over the WRB, which means each upper layer overlaps the lower one to prevent water from entering the wall cavity.
4. **Seal and Tape**: The top edge of the metal flashing is secured using roofing or siding nails, and the WRB flap is folded down over it. The ends of the flap and any slits on the sides are sealed with flashing tape to complete the waterproofing assembly.
5. **Inspect for Quality**: Finally, the installation is inspected to ensure that all components are properly integrated and that there are no gaps or misalignments that could allow water penetration.

By following these steps, contractors create a continuous barrier that directs water away from the building, ensuring the deck junctions are well-protected against moisture intrusion.

Common metal flashing materials used at deck junctions include:

- **Aluminum**: Known for its lightweight and corrosion-resistant properties.
- **Copper**: Offers excellent durability and a long lifespan.
- **Galvanized Steel**: Steel coated with a layer of zinc to prevent rusting.
- **Stainless Steel**: Highly resistant to corrosion and staining.

These materials are chosen for their ability to withstand the elements and provide a reliable seal against water intrusion.

When selecting metal flashings for coastal environments, several important considerations come into play to ensure long-term durability and corrosion resistance:

1. **Corrosion Resistance**: Choose materials that are inherently resistant to corrosion, such as aluminum or stainless steel.
2. **Protective Coatings**: Utilize protective coatings like Kynar or Flurothane paint to slow down the corrosion process.
3. **Environmental Factors**: Consider the specific coastal conditions, such as proximity to breaking surf, rainfall, and salt spray, which can influence the severity of the environment and the type of maintenance required[1].
4. **Design Considerations**: opt for profiles that allow for good water drainage and minimize standing water, which can accelerate corrosion.
5. **Installation Techniques**: Ensure correct installation techniques to prevent corrosion from salty sea spray, including proper storage and handling of materials.
6. **Compatibility**: Be mindful of dissimilar metals and their potential for galvanic corrosion. Select fasteners and accessories that are compatible with the chosen metal flashing.

By carefully considering these factors, you can select metal flashings that will withstand the harsh conditions of coastal environments and provide reliable performance over time.

To prevent galvanic corrosion between dissimilar metals in flashing systems, it's important to consider the following measures:

1. **Insulation**: Place a non-conductive material between the contact points of the coupling metals to break the electrical path.
2. **Electrolyte Isolation**: Prevent contact with electrolytes by using water-repellent compounds or coatings.
3. **Appropriate Metal Selection**: Choose metals that are close together in the galvanic series (Galvanic Corrosion scale) to minimize potential difference.
4. **Corrosion Inhibitors**: Apply corrosion inhibitors to the metals to reduce the corrosion rate.
5. **Minimizing Area Ratio**: Keep the area ratio of the cathode to the anode as low as possible to decrease the corrosion impact on the anode.

By implementing these strategies, you can significantly reduce the risk of galvanic corrosion in metal flashing systems.

Chapter Summary: Key Takeaways for Effective Waterproofing

Strategic Considerations:

- **Critical Junctions**: Identifying and protecting critical junctions and transitions is essential to prevent water ingress.
- **Flashing Components**: The selection of flashing components must be tailored to the specific needs of each junction, choosing between rigid metal and flexible sheet membranes.
- **WRB Integration**: A meticulous plan for integrating flashings with the Weather Resistant Barrier (WRB) is necessary to create a seamless moisture barrier.
- **Roof and Wall Flashings**: These should be designed to work together, providing comprehensive protection against water.
- **Material Compatibility**: Ensuring chemical compatibility among all materials used is crucial to prevent degradation and ensure the longevity of the waterproofing system.

Refined Construction Activities:

- **Window Flashing**: Must be applied with precision and fully integrated with the WRB, adhering to guidelines from designers or manufacturers.
- **Installation Principles**: Fundamental principles include maintaining WRB continuity, sealing for air leakage, ensuring proper alignment, and facilitating water drainage.

- **Industry Standards**: Compliance with standards such as AAMA 2400 and ASTM e2112-07 is critical, with any deviations addressed through RFIs.
- **Dupont Tyvek**: Recognized for providing comprehensive window installation details.

Advanced Flashing Techniques:

- **Shingle Fashion**: Flashing components should be integrated in a shingle fashion for effective water shedding.
- **Advanced Methods**: Use of multi-part sill pans, through-wall flashings, and corner reinforcements enhance the waterproofing system.
- **Swing Door Flashing**: Follows similar principles of shingle lapping, corner reinforcement, and the use of compatible sealants.

Installation Locations:

- **Optimal Protection**: Metal and flexible flashings are installed at strategic locations such as deck and roof junctions, material transitions, wall penetrations, and around openings.
- **Coordinated Efforts**: Achieving a watertight exterior requires the collaboration of various professionals including window installers, framers, siders, roofers, and sheet metal subcontractors.

By adhering to these key takeaways, construction professionals can ensure robust waterproofing measures are in place, safeguarding buildings against potential water damage and contributing to their overall durability and integrity.

Chapter Eight: Roof Assemblies

"No house should ever be on a hill or on anything. It should be of the hill. Belonging to it. Hill and house should live together each the happier for the other."

Frank Lloyd Wright

When it comes to constructing a robust roof, strategic planning and precision are key. A well-assembled roof not only provides shelter but also enhances the architectural integrity and longevity of a building. Here's an essential guide to understanding the complexities of roof assemblies and ensuring your roof stands the test of time.

Understanding Diverse Roof Systems Roof assemblies are not one-size-fits-all; they vary to accommodate different roof slopes and architectural designs. Whether it's a steep slope that calls for shingles or a flat roof that requires sheet membranes, each system is tailored to meet specific structural requirements and aesthetic preferences.

Choosing the Right Topping Materials The top layer of a roof is its first line of defense against the elements. Common materials include asphalt shingles, clay or concrete tiles, and thermoplastic olefin (TPO) or polyvinyl chloride (PVC) membranes for low slope roofs. Each material offers unique benefits, from the classic look of tiles to the modern efficiency of membrane systems.

Managing Anomalies for Effective Water Drainage Special attention must be paid to dead valleys and other architectural features that can disrupt water flow. Proper management of these anomalies is crucial to ensure effective water drainage and maintain the structural integrity of the roof.

Ensuring Material Compatibility The chemical compatibility of all materials used in the roof assembly is vital. Incompatible materials can react with one another, leading to premature degradation and potential roof failure. It's essential to select materials that will work in harmony over the long term.

Assessing Moisture Content Moisture trapped in the roof deck can lead to mold growth and material decay. Assessing the moisture content before installation is crucial to prevent these issues and ensure the longevity of the roof.

Strategic Considerations for Robust Roof Assemblies:

- **Diverse Systems**: Roof assemblies can vary, with systems chosen based on roof slope and specific architectural requirements.
- **Topping Materials**: Common materials for the top layer include asphalt shingles, clay or concrete tiles, and membranes like TPO or PVC for low slope roofs.
- **Anomaly Management**: Special attention must be given to dead valleys and other unique features to ensure proper water drainage and structural integrity.
- **Material Compatibility**: The chemical compatibility of all materials used in the roof assembly is vital to prevent reactions that could compromise the roof's durability.
- **Moisture Assessment**: Determining the moisture content of the roof deck is crucial to prevent trapped moisture, which can lead to mold growth and material decay.

Refined Construction Activities for Roof Flashing:

- **Confined Rake Integration**: Channel and counter flashings are carefully integrated at confined rakes to prevent water ingress.
- **Sidewall Terminations**: Include diverter or "kick out" flashings at the confined rake terminations to direct water away from the wall and into the gutter system.
- **Valley Metal Installation**: Valley metal is installed over a protective layer of underlayment, a practice especially common in tile roof systems.
- **Headwall Flashing**: The integration of headwall flashing is critical for the roof-to-wall transition, ensuring a watertight seal.

Roof Types and Their Characteristics:

- **Roof Dormer**: The term "dormer" refers to the window, while the structure containing it is known as a gablet. A dormer window is typically a double-hung unit.

- **Gable Roof**: The triangular area and trim of a gable roof are collectively referred to as a pediment.
- **Hip Roof**: Characterized by terra cotta roof tiles, often referred to as Spanish Tile roofs, with notable hip and ridge caps and exposed rafter tails under the fascia.
- **Gambrel Roof**: Recognizable by its gambrel style, often complicated by the addition of shed dormers originating from the roof's knuckle joint.

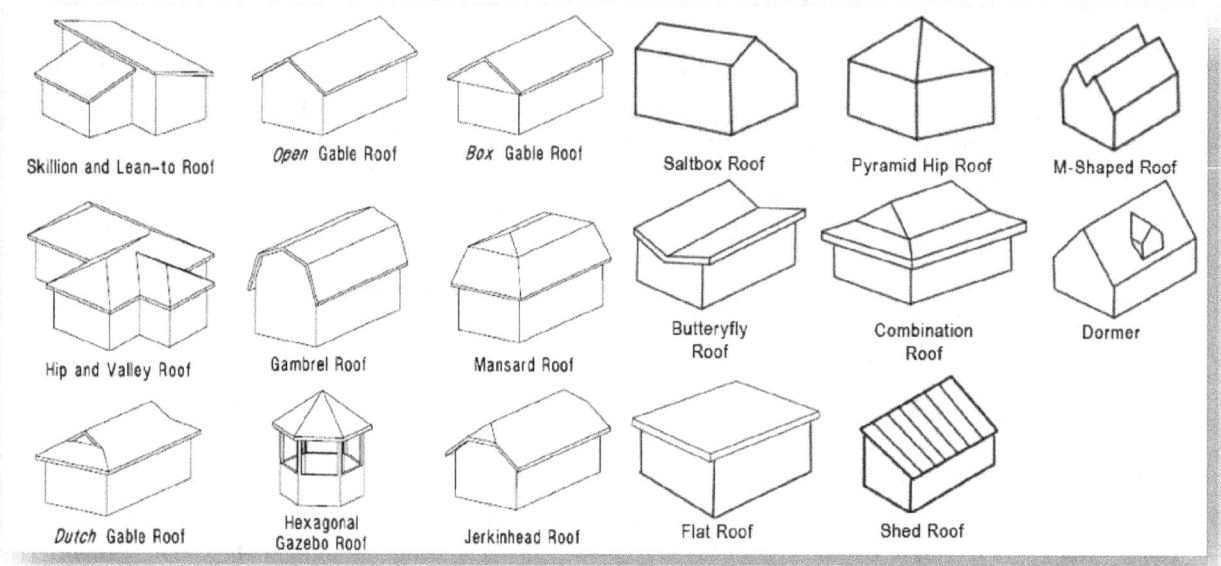

Different Roof Styles.

Tile Roof System Overview:

- **Waterproofing Foundation**: The installation begins with fundamental waterproofing, followed by the roofing material:
    - Underlayment
    - Battens
    - Static venting provisions
    - 2X members
    - Tile

This enhanced chapter provides a detailed guide to constructing durable and effective roof assemblies, emphasizing the importance of strategic planning, material selection, and meticulous installation practices to ensure long-lasting protection from the elements.

Roof flashing is a critical component in any roofing system, designed to prevent water from entering the structure at joints or penetrations. Here's a detailed look at the different types of roof flashings:

1. **Valley Flashing**: Installed in the valleys where two roof planes meet, valley flashing directs water away from these vulnerable areas.
2. **Drip Edge Flashing**: This type is placed along the edges of the roof to guide water into the gutters, protecting the fascia and underlying wood.
3. **Vent Pipe Flashing**: Also known as boot flashing, it seals around vent pipes protruding through the roof to prevent leaks.
4. **Step Flashing**: Used where a roof meets a vertical wall or sidewall, such as around chimneys or dormers, installed in a step pattern to ensure proper water flow.
5. **Apron Flashing**: Often used in conjunction with step flashing around chimneys and dormer windows, it provides an additional layer of protection against water intrusion.
6. **Metal Flashing**: Made from materials like aluminum, steel, or copper, metal flashing is durable and flexible, commonly used due to its longevity and effectiveness.
7. **Copper Flashing**: Known for its superior durability and resistance to corrosion, copper flashing is a premium choice that can last for decades.

Each type of flashing serves a specific purpose and is chosen based on the needs of the roof's design and the environmental conditions it must withstand. Proper installation and maintenance of roof flashing are essential to ensure the longevity and integrity of the roofing system. If you're considering a roofing project, it's important to consult with a professional to determine the best types of flashing for your needs.

During roof flashing installation, it's important to avoid several common mistakes to ensure a watertight seal and the longevity of the roof. Here are some key errors to avoid:

1. **Improper Installation**: Not following the manufacturer's guidelines for proper flashing installation can lead to weak points where water can seep through.
2. **Inadequate Sealant Application**: Neglecting to apply enough sealant can compromise the flashing's ability to create a watertight seal.
3. **Incorrect Material Choice**: Choosing the wrong type of flashing material for the specific roofing application can result in premature deterioration and leaks.
4. **Inadequate Step Flashing**: Failing to install enough step flashing or improperly placing it can lead to water penetration.
5. **Neglecting Counter Flashing**: Omitting counter flashing or installing it incorrectly can leave your roof vulnerable to leaks.
6. **Poorly Installed Valley Flashing**: Improper installation of valley flashing can result in water seepage, especially in areas prone to water accumulation.
7. **Using the Wrong Fasteners**: Utilizing incorrect or incompatible fasteners may compromise the flashing's integrity.
8. **Overlooking Drip Edge Installation**: Drip edges are crucial in directing water away from the roof, and improper installation can lead to water infiltration.

9. **Ignoring Roof Pitch Considerations**: Failing to account for the roof pitch during flashing installation can result in inadequate water drainage and increased risk of leaks.
10. **Improperly Installed Skylight Flashing**: Skylights require special attention during flashing installation, and incorrect installation can lead to leaks.
11. **Neglecting Chimney Flashing**: Chimneys are common sources of leaks, so ensure proper installation of chimney flashing, paying attention to details such as counter flashing and sealant application.
12. **Skipping Roof Inspection**: Failure to conduct a thorough roof inspection before flashing installation can lead to overlooking existing issues that may compromise the effectiveness of the flashing.
13. **Incorrectly Installed Kickout Flashing**: Kickout flashing is crucial for preventing water from infiltrating the wall at the point where the roof meets a sidewall.

It's crucial to follow best practices and guidelines for roof flashing installation, and when in doubt, consult with or hire a professional roofer to ensure the job is done correctly. Proper installation will protect your roof and home from water damage and potentially costly repairs in the future.

Chapter Summary: Key Takeaways for Robust Roof Assemblies

Strategic Considerations:

- **Diverse Systems**: Roof assemblies must be tailored to accommodate varying slopes and architectural designs, ensuring structural integrity and aesthetic alignment.
- **Topping Materials**: The selection of top layer materials, such as asphalt shingles, clay, or concrete tiles, and TPO or PVC membranes, is crucial for the roof's performance and longevity.
- **Anomaly Management**: Identifying and addressing anomalies like dead valleys is essential for effective water drainage and maintaining structural integrity.
- **Material Compatibility**: Ensuring the chemical compatibility of all roofing materials is vital to prevent adverse reactions that could weaken the roof.
- **Moisture Assessment**: Assessing the moisture content of the roof deck is necessary to prevent issues like mold growth and material decay.

Refined Construction Activities:

- **Confined Rake Integration**: Proper integration of channel and counter flashings at confined rakes is key to preventing water ingress.
- **Sidewall Terminations**: The use of diverter or "kick out" flashings at sidewall terminations is important to direct water into the gutter system and away from the wall.

- **Valley Metal Installation**: Installing valley metal over a protective layer of underlayment is a common practice, particularly in tile roof systems, to enhance water shedding.
- **Headwall Flashing**: Integrating headwall flashing is critical for a watertight roof-to-wall transition.

Roof Types and Characteristics:

- **Roof Dormer**: A dormer, typically a double-hung window, adds space and light, while the gablet structure adds architectural interest.
- **Gable Roof**: Known for its triangular shape, the pediment of a gable roof is a defining feature.
- **Hip Roof**: Often covered with terra cotta tiles, the hip roof is distinguished by its Spanish influence and decorative hip and ridge caps.
- **Gambrel Roof**: The gambrel style is notable for its unique shape and the complexity added by shed dormers.

Tile Roof System Overview:

- **Waterproofing Foundation**: The roofing process starts with fundamental waterproofing, followed by the installation of underlayment, battens, static venting provisions, 2X members, and tiles, ensuring a durable and weather-resistant roof assembly.

By adhering to these key considerations and refined construction practices, builders can ensure that roof assemblies are not only aesthetically pleasing but also functionally robust and durable.

MacIntyre/Residential Construction: understanding the Basics.

Chapter Nine: Exterior Cladding and Assemblies

"The supreme art of war is to subdue the enemy without fighting. In the same way, the supreme art of building is to protect without the need for repair."

Sun Tzu

In the dynamic world of architectural design, the building envelope serves as the critical interface between the comfort of the indoors and the elements outside. Enhanced exterior cladding and assemblies are revolutionizing this interface, offering superior protection, energy efficiency, and aesthetic appeal.

The Role of Enhanced Cladding in Modern Architecture

Exterior cladding is no longer just a shield against weather; it's a sophisticated system that contributes to the building's energy performance and visual identity. Innovations in materials and installation techniques have led to the development of cladding solutions that are both functional and strikingly beautiful. From sleek metal panels to eco-friendly composite materials, the options available today cater to a wide range of preferences and requirements.

Strategic Integration for Optimal Performance

The integration of cladding elements with the rest of the building envelope is a strategic process. It involves careful consideration of thermal insulation, moisture management, and ventilation. Advanced systems now feature integrated layers that work cohesively to regulate indoor temperatures, prevent water ingress, and allow buildings to 'breathe.' This holistic approach ensures that the envelope performs efficiently throughout the year, reducing the need for artificial heating and cooling.

Sustainability at the Forefront

Sustainability is a driving force in the evolution of exterior cladding. Materials are being chosen not only for their durability and maintenance requirements but also for their environmental impact. Recycled content, renewable sources, and life-cycle assessments are becoming standard considerations in the selection process. Moreover, cladding systems are increasingly designed to be recyclable at the end of their life, contributing to a circular economy in the construction industry.

Technological Advancements in Cladding Assemblies

Technology plays a pivotal role in the enhanced performance of cladding systems. Smart membranes that adapt to humidity levels, self-cleaning surfaces, and photovoltaic cladding that generates electricity are just a few examples of how technology is being integrated into exteriors. These features not only improve the building's performance but also reduce maintenance costs and contribute to energy generation.

Aesthetic Innovation and Customization

The aesthetic possibilities of enhanced cladding are limitless. Digital fabrication techniques allow for intricate patterns, custom textures, and a vast array of colors. This level of customization enables architects and designers to create unique facades that reflect the building's identity and blend harmoniously with their surroundings.

Enhanced Cladding for Health and Comfort

The health and comfort of occupants are paramount in the design of modern building envelopes. Enhanced cladding systems contribute to a healthier indoor environment by managing air and moisture flow, filtering out pollutants, and reducing noise transmission. By prioritizing these aspects, buildings not only become more comfortable but also support the well-being of those who use them.

The Future of Cladding: Smart and Adaptive

The future of exterior cladding is smart and adaptive. As buildings become more integrated with technology, cladding systems will evolve to be even more responsive to environmental changes and user needs. The potential for facades that change color with the weather, generate energy on demand, and repair themselves is on the horizon.

Enhanced exterior cladding and assemblies are at the forefront of building technology, offering solutions that are sustainable, efficient, and visually captivating. As we embrace these advancements, the buildings of tomorrow will not only stand as structures of shelter but also as embodiments of innovation and environmental stewardship.

Key Considerations:

- **Exterior Finishes**: Installation should align with project plans and specifications.
- **Material Coordination**: The siding/stucco subcontractor and general contractor must synchronize the delivery of cladding and trim materials.
- **Common Exterior Finishes**: These include stucco cladding, fiber cement siding, wood siding, and vinyl cladding.
- **Trim Integration**: Trim members, such as SPF, EPS, PVC, and Fiber Cement, are integrated into most systems.
- **Veneer Application**: Exterior walls may be adorned with veneers that mimic natural stone or traditional brick pavers.
- **Cladding Application**: Proper application of exterior cladding components is crucial for structural protection.

Construction Activities:

- **Stucco Application**: The building code requires the exterior wall to be water-resistant and capable of managing incidental water infiltration, with some codes specifying a minimum drainage capacity.

Concealed Barrier Overview:

- **Water-Resistant Barrier (WRB)**: Installed in a shingle-lap manner, with flashings allowing drainage and integration with weep screeds.
- **Drainage Mat**: Utilized alongside a sacrificial WRB layer to facilitate water management.
- **Rain Screen**: Incorporates pressure equalization and through-wall flashings, with battens spaced over studs for optimal performance.
- **Drain Mat**: Must be sturdy enough to withstand lath installation without being compromised.

Stucco Cladding Details:

- **Three Coat Stucco**: Comprises a 7/8" thick layer, including scratch, brown, and finish coats, with various finish options like colored, acrylic, or elastomeric finishes.
- **Control and Expansion Joints**: Essential for managing stucco movement around windows, doors, and floor lines, ensuring the integration of accessory flanges and proper sealant application.

Siding and Trim Considerations:

- **Concealed Barrier Principles**: Follows the same principles as stucco, with WRB and through-wall flashings forming the foundation.
- **Siding Types**: Selection includes Clapboard, Dolly Varden, Bevel, T&G, Rustic Vee, Shiplap, Channel Rustic, and Board & Batten.
- **Exposure**: The amount of siding exposed versus the horizontal overlap is typically between 4" to 12", with 6" being a popular choice.
- **Trim Installation**: Fiber cement or wood trim members are installed prior to siding, ensuring proper alignment and integration.

This chapter has been enhanced to provide a comprehensive understanding of exterior cladding and assemblies, emphasizing the importance of following building codes, coordinating material delivery, and applying proper construction techniques to ensure a durable and water-resistant exterior.

Adhered Masonry Veneers:

- **Diverse Styles**: A vast array of pre-manufactured adhered masonry veneers are available, offering various styles to suit different architectural aesthetics.
- **Stucco Similarity**: The installation process up to the scratch coat stage mirrors that of stucco, ensuring a familiar method for contractors.
- **Mortar Application**: Masonry units are "buttered" with mortar on their backs and then firmly adhered to the grooved scratch coat, creating a strong bond.

Mechanically Attached Brick Veneer:

- **Drainage Space**: A 1-inch gap is maintained between the drainage plane and the backside of the brick pavers, facilitating proper moisture management.
- **Through-Wall Flashings**: Similar to adhered masonry, through-wall flashings are installed to direct incidental water out of the wall assembly.
- **Mortar Catch**: While a drain mat is not typically used, many masons opt to install a mortar catch to prevent mortar droppings from clogging the weep holes.
- **Mechanical Attachment**: Brick pavers are securely attached using metal ties and steel lintels, especially over openings, to ensure structural stability and durability.

This section on brick and stone veneer provides a clear and detailed guide to the selection and installation of veneer systems, emphasizing the importance of proper techniques and materials to achieve a durable and visually appealing exterior cladding.

Working with veneers can present several challenges, even for experienced woodworkers. Here are some common issues that may arise:

1. **Buckling and Warping**: Veneers can buckle or warp due to changes in humidity or if they are not stored properly before use.
2. **Delamination**: This occurs when the veneer separates from the substrate. It can be caused by inadequate adhesive, improper pressing, or tension within the veneer.
3. **Seam Separation**: If veneers are not joined correctly, the seams may become visible or separate over time, affecting the finish.
4. **Color Matching**: Achieving a consistent color across different veneer sheets can be difficult, especially when dealing with natural wood that has inherent variations.
5. **Adhesive Issues**: Selecting the right adhesive is crucial. Some adhesives may not bond well with certain veneer types or may cause bleed-through, which can stain the veneer surface.
6. **Substrate Preparation**: The surface to which the veneer is applied must be prepared correctly to ensure a good bond. This may include sanding or sealing the substrate.
7. **Cutting and Trimming**: Veneers are thin and fragile, making them challenging to cut and trim without causing splits or chips.
8. **Repairing Damage**: Veneers can be damaged during handling or installation. Repairing them requires skill to ensure the fix is not noticeable.
9. **Application on Curved Surfaces**: Applying veneers to curved or complex shapes requires special techniques and can be more challenging than working with flat surfaces.

To overcome these challenges, it's important to follow best practices, such as proper acclimatization of veneers, using the right tools and adhesives, and ensuring a clean, stable work environment. Additionally, patience and attention to detail are key in achieving a high-quality finish with veneers.

Preventing veneer delamination during installation involves several key steps to ensure a strong, lasting bond:

1. **Proper Substrate Preparation**: Ensure the substrate is clean, dry, and smooth. Any debris or moisture can compromise the adhesive's effectiveness.
2. **Correct Adhesive Selection**: Use the right type of adhesive for the veneer material. Some adhesives are specifically formulated for veneer application and can resist moisture and heat better.
3. **Climate Control**: Maintain a stable environment with controlled humidity and temperature during and after installation to prevent the veneer from expanding or contracting excessively.
4. **Adequate Pressing**: Apply even pressure across the veneer during installation to ensure good contact with the substrate. Use a veneer press or clamps for larger pieces.
5. **Avoid Overheating**: If using a heat-activated adhesive, be careful not to overheat the veneer, as this can cause the glue to fail and lead to delamination.

6. **Proper Fastening**: When using nails or screws, place them at least ¾ inch away from the edges to prevent the veneer from splitting or lifting.
7. **Sealing Edges**: Seal the edges of the veneer to protect against moisture ingress, which can cause swelling and eventual delamination.
8. **Ventilation**: Ensure adequate ventilation in the area where the veneer is installed to allow any moisture to escape and prevent it from getting trapped.

By following these guidelines, you can significantly reduce the risk of veneer delamination and ensure a durable finish for your project.

Chapter Summary: Key Takeaways on Enhanced Exterior Wall Cladding and Assemblies

Key Considerations for Installation:

- **Exterior Finishes**: Align installation with project plans and specifications for a cohesive design and structural integrity.
- **Material Coordination**: Ensure timely delivery of cladding and trim materials through effective coordination between subcontractors and the general contractor.
- **Common Finishes**: Include versatile options like stucco cladding, fiber cement siding, wood siding, and vinyl cladding to cater to different aesthetic and functional needs.
- **Trim Integration**: Incorporate trim members such as SPF, EPS, PVC, and Fiber Cement into cladding systems for enhanced detail and finish.
- **Veneer Application**: Use veneers that replicate natural stone or brick pavers for a sophisticated exterior appearance.
- **Cladding Application**: Proper application is essential for the structural protection and longevity of the cladding.

   Construction Activities and Techniques:

- **Stucco Application**: Comply with building codes requiring water-resistant exterior walls and manage incidental water infiltration effectively.
- **Concealed Barrier**: Install a Water-Resistant Barrier (WRB) in a shingle-lap manner, with flashings for drainage and weep screeds integration.
- **Drainage Solutions**: Use drainage mats and rain screens to facilitate water management and ensure the durability of the wall system.
- **Stucco Cladding**: Apply a three-coat stucco system with various finish options and ensure proper control and expansion joints for movement management.

   Siding and Trim Details:

- **Concealed Barrier Principles**: Apply the same principles as stucco for WRB and flashing integration.

- **Siding Types**: Offer a variety of siding types such as Clapboard, Bevel, and Board & Batten for diverse architectural styles.
- **Exposure**: Determine the exposure level of siding to balance aesthetics with protection.
- **Trim Installation**: Install trim members before siding for a seamless finish and proper alignment.

Adhered and Mechanically Attached Veneers:

- **Adhered Masonry Veneers**: Provide a selection of pre-manufactured veneers and ensure a strong bond with proper mortar application.
- **Mechanically Attached Brick Veneer**: Maintain a drainage space, use through-wall flashings, and secure brick pavers with metal ties and steel lintels for a durable veneer solution.

This chapter emphasizes the importance of meticulous planning, material selection, and precise installation practices in creating durable, water-resistant, and aesthetically pleasing exterior wall claddings and assemblies. By adhering to these key takeaways, builders and designers can ensure high-quality outcomes that stand the test of time.

Chapter Ten: Interior Finishes Part 1

"When we build, let us think that we build forever. Let it not be for present delight nor for present use alone. Let it be such work as our descendants will thank us for."

John Ruskin

Insulation and Fire Safety: Ensuring energy efficiency and comfort in a building starts with the right insulation choice. Whether it's blown-in or batt insulation, identifying the correct R-values is crucial for maintaining temperature control and reducing energy costs. Fire caulking plays a pivotal role in safety, sealing gaps to prevent the spread of fire and smoke, thereby protecting the building's occupants and structure.

Pre-Coverage Inspection: Before the walls are sealed, a meticulous re-inspection of Mechanical, Electrical, and Plumbing (MEP) systems is imperative. This step is the contractor's last opportunity to address any issues, ensuring that all systems are correctly installed and functioning as intended.

Interior Finish Essentials: The installation of gypsum panels forms the basis of interior finishes, creating fire-rated assemblies tailored to project specifications. The selection of textures and paints is guided by design documents, contributing to the desired aesthetic appeal. A review of interior trim locations and types is essential to ensure they complement the overall design scheme. Floor finishes and treatments, such as countertops or plumbing finishes, are chosen in collaboration with the design team or the owner, adding the final touches to the building's interior.

Construction Activities: Gypsum wall board installation is a critical construction activity. After completing the upper-level ceiling drywall, attic insulation is blown in to conserve energy. The gypsum wall board is then installed according to architectural specifications, providing necessary fire ratings, sound dampening, and structural rigidity. Drywall finishing involves taping seams, applying joint compound, sanding, and texturing to achieve a smooth and ready-to-paint surface.

Fire Rated Assembly Details: Fire-rated assemblies are integral to building safety, designed to withstand fire exposure for a specified time without structural failure or allowing fire passage. These assemblies include materials like fire-retardant-treated lumber and gypsum board, and their performance is validated through testing and certification by organizations such as Underwriters Laboratories (UL). Compliance with International Code Council (ICC) mandates and ASTM standards is non-negotiable, ensuring that fire-rated assemblies meet the highest safety requirements.

Interior Trim Installation: The installation of interior trim, including window and door trims, baseboards, crown molding, and other specialty trim assemblies, follows the texturing of drywall. This phase also includes the installation of pre-hung doors, specialty paneling, and built-in cabinetry. All trim joints are caulked in preparation for painting, contributing to the polished look of the interior.

Final Finishes: The final finishes bring the interior space to life. Fixtures such as showers, sinks, and lavatories are installed, plumbing and heating systems are set up, and the water heater is connected to the fixtures. MEP finishing touches include the installation of light fixtures, faucets, and safety devices like fire and carbon monoxide detectors, ensuring the interior setup is complete and functional.

This chapter outlines a comprehensive approach to executing interior finishes, emphasizing quality, safety, and aesthetic coherence. By adhering to these guidelines, contractors can ensure a polished and secure living environment, ready for occupancy and daily use.

Insulation and Fire Safety:

- **Insulation Choices**: Selecting the right insulation, whether blown-in or batt, is crucial. It's important to identify the appropriate R-values to ensure energy efficiency and comfort.
- **Fire Caulking**: Implement draft stop and final fire caulking to seal gaps and prevent the spread of fire and smoke.

Pre-Coverage Inspection:

- **MEP Re-Inspection**: Before covering the walls, a thorough re-inspection of Mechanical, Electrical, and Plumbing (MEP) systems is essential to address any potential issues.

Interior Finish Essentials:

- **Gypsum Panel Installation**: Gypsum panels are installed to meet project-specific fire-rated assembly requirements.
- **Texture and Paint**: Select and order textures and paints as per design documents to achieve the desired aesthetic.
- **Trim and Finish Review**: Assess interior trim locations and types, ensuring they align with the overall design scheme.
- **Floor and Treatment Selection**: Choose floor finishes and treatments like countertops or plumbing finishes in collaboration with the design team or the owner.

Construction Activities:

- **Gypsum Wall Board Installation**: After completing the upper-level ceiling drywall, blow in attic insulation to conserve energy. Install gypsum wall board as per architectural specifications, providing fire ratings, sound dampening, and structural rigidity.
- **Drywall Finishing**: Tape all drywall seams, apply joint compound, sand the joints upon curing, and apply the chosen texture.

Fire Rated Assembly Details:

- **Compliance**: Ensure fire-resistance ratings meet ICC mandates and ASTM standards.
- **UL Rated Assemblies**: Utilize assemblies designed by Underwriters Laboratories with specific UL numbers, as they have been tested and proven to comply with ASTM standards.

  ### Interior Trim Installation:

- **Trim Work**: After texturing the drywall, install trim pieces including window and door trims, baseboards, crown molding, and other specialty trim assemblies.
- **Door and Cabinetry**: Install pre-hung doors, specialty paneling, and built-in cabinetry, caulking all trim joints in preparation for painting.

Final Finishes:

- **Fixture Installation**: Install interior finishes such as showers, sinks, and lavatories.
- **Plumbing and Heating**: Set up the water heater and connect all plumbing to the fixtures.

- **MEP Finishing Touches**: Install finish MEP items like light fixtures, faucets, and fire/carbon monoxide detectors to complete the interior setup.

This chapter provides a detailed framework for executing interior finishes with an emphasis on quality, safety, and aesthetic coherence, ensuring a polished and secure living environment.

Fire-rated assemblies are crucial components in building construction that provide a specified degree of fire resistance. They are designed to contain and prevent the spread of fire within a building for a certain period, typically ranging from one to four hours. Here's an overview of their key aspects:

1. **Fire Resistance**: This refers to the time an assembly can withstand a standard fire exposure, as defined by ASTM E119, without losing its structural integrity or allowing the passage of fire.
2. **Components**: Fire-rated assemblies can include a variety of materials such as fire-retardant-treated lumber, gypsum board, insulation batts, and specific types of fasteners. The configuration of these materials is critical to the assembly's performance.
3. **Testing and Certification**: Assemblies are tested by organizations like Underwriters Laboratories (UL) and are given a UL number. These tests ensure that the assemblies meet the required fire-resistance ratings according to ASTM standards.
4. **Building Codes**: The International Code Council (ICC) mandates that fire-resistance ratings comply with certain ASTM standards to ensure safety and compliance in building designs.
5. **Applications**: Fire-rated assemblies are used in walls, floors, and ceilings to compartmentalize a building into fire zones, which helps in containing fires and allowing occupants more time to evacuate safely.
6. **Acoustical Performance**: Some fire-rated assemblies also provide sound dampening properties, which is an added benefit in multi-unit residential or commercial buildings.

By incorporating these assemblies into the design and construction of buildings, architects and builders aim to enhance the safety of occupants and protect property in the event of a fire. It's important to consult with professionals and adhere to local building codes when selecting and installing fire-rated assemblies.

Final finishes in construction refer to the last phase of the building process where the interior is completed and made ready for occupancy. Here's a detailed look at each aspect:

Fixture Installation:

- **Interior Finishes**: This involves installing fixtures that are part of the building's permanent interior, such as showers, sinks, and lavatories.

- **Aesthetic and Functional**: These fixtures not only serve functional purposes but also contribute to the aesthetic appeal of the interior space.

Plumbing and Heating:

- **Water Heater Setup**: The installation of the water heater is a critical step, ensuring that hot water is available throughout the building.
- **Plumbing Connections**: All plumbing fixtures are connected to the water supply lines and drainage systems to ensure proper functionality.

MEP Finishing Touches:

- **Lighting**: Installing light fixtures is a key part of MEP finishing touches, providing illumination, and contributing to the ambiance of the space.
- **Faucets**: Faucets are installed at sinks, showers, and other areas requiring water access.
- **Safety Devices**: Fire and carbon monoxide detectors are installed to ensure the safety of the building's occupants.

These final touches are essential for making the space livable and ensuring that all systems are operational and meet the required safety standards. The completion of these tasks marks the end of the construction process, and the building is then ready for furniture, occupants, and use.

Chapter Summary: Interior Finishes Pat 1

Insulation and Fire Safety:

- **Right Insulation Choice**: Selecting the appropriate insulation with the correct R-values is essential for energy efficiency and temperature control.
- **Fire Caulking**: Vital for safety, it seals gaps to prevent the spread of fire and smoke, protecting occupants and the building's structure.

Pre-Coverage Inspection:

- **MEP Systems Re-inspection**: A thorough re-inspection of Mechanical, Electrical, and Plumbing systems is conducted before sealing the walls to ensure proper installation and functionality.

Interior Finish Essentials:

- **Gypsum Panels**: Form the basis of interior finishes, contributing to fire-rated assemblies that meet project specifications.
- **Textures and Paints**: Chosen based on design documents, they enhance the aesthetic appeal.

- **Interior Trim Review**: Ensures that trim locations and types align with the overall design scheme.
- **Floor Finishes and Treatments**: Selected collaboratively to add the final touches to the building's interior.

Construction Activities:

- **Gypsum Wall Board Installation**: Provides fire ratings, sound dampening, and structural rigidity.
- **Drywall Finishing**: Involves taping, applying joint compound, sanding, and texturing for a smooth surface.

Fire Rated Assembly Details:

- **Fire-Resistant Materials**: Include treated lumber and gypsum board, certified by organizations like UL.
- **Compliance**: Adherence to ICC mandates and ASTM standards ensures the highest safety requirements.

Interior Trim Installation:

- **Trim and Specialty Assemblies**: Installed post-texturing, including window and door trims, baseboards, and crown molding.
- **Pre-Hung Doors and Cabinetry**: Added before painting, contributing to the interior's polished look.

Final Finishes:

- **Installation of Fixtures**: Showers, sinks, lavatories, and connection of plumbing and heating systems.
- **MEP Finishing Touches**: Light fixtures, faucets, and safety devices are installed to complete the functional interior setup.

This chapter emphasizes the importance of quality, safety, and aesthetic coherence in executing interior finishes, ensuring a polished and secure living environment ready for occupancy. Contractors adhering to these guidelines can deliver a home that is both beautiful and safe for daily use.

Chapter Eleven: Interior Finishes Part 2

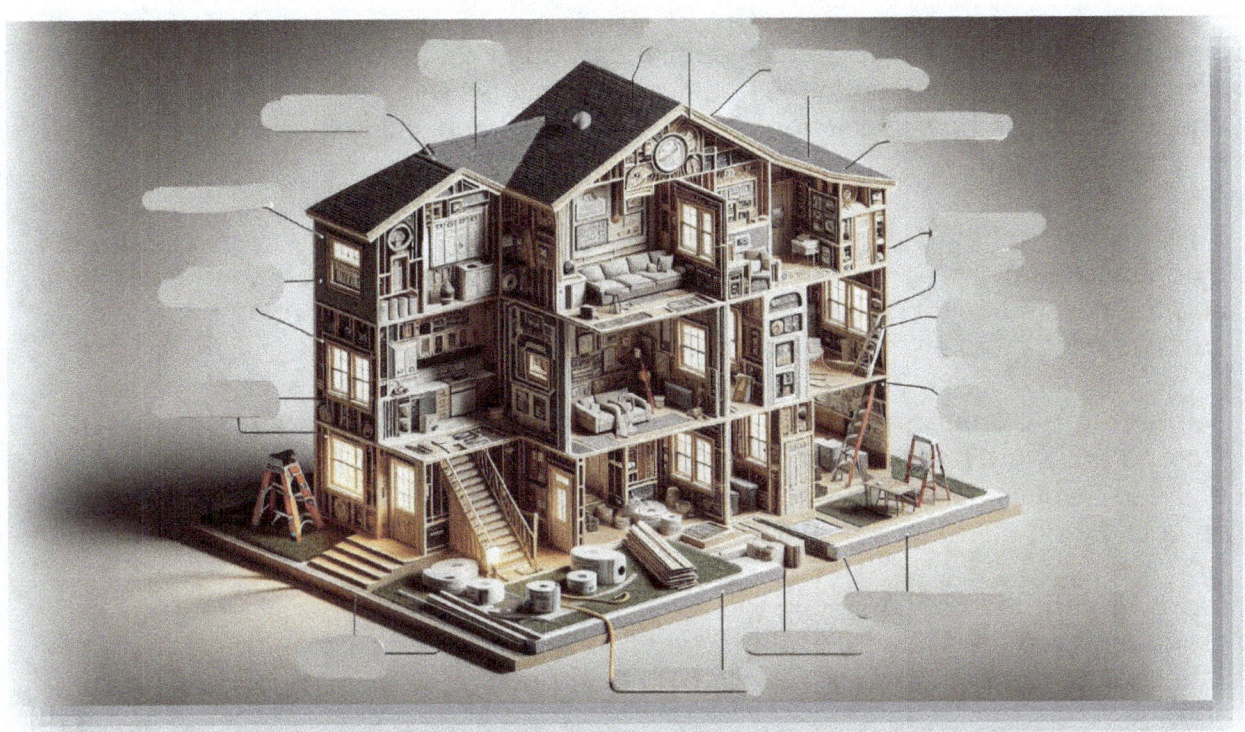

"Architecture is an imitation of nature. As birds and bees built their nests, so humans construct houses to protect themselves from the elements."

Vitruvius

As the construction journey nears its end, Chapter Eleven focuses on the final stages of interior finishes, marking the transition from a construction site to a homeowner's sanctuary. This chapter outlines the meticulous process of adding the last touches that transform a house into a home.

Homeowner Turnover Considerations: The home is on the cusp of being handed over to the homeowner. This pivotal moment is preceded by a final walkthrough, where the builder's sales representative and the future homeowner meticulously review every finish, ensuring that every detail aligns with the homeowner's vision and the home's design specifications.

Final Construction Activities: The last phase of construction activities is characterized by the installation of cabinets and countertops, the embodiment of the home's functionality and style. These elements are carefully selected to reflect the homeowner's taste and the home's overall design theme.

Flooring Installation: Following the completion of the wall finishes, the installation of the finish floor commences. This includes laying down tile, wood, carpet, or linoleum as per the design documents. The choice of flooring material plays a significant role in the home's ambiance, comfort, and acoustic properties.

Appliance Connection: Essential appliances, such as the dishwasher and microwave, are connected to their designated outlets. This step is crucial for ensuring that the home's kitchen is fully operational and ready for the homeowner to use from day one.

Final Construction Clean: The culmination of the construction process is marked by a thorough clean-up. This final construction clean is not just about removing dust and debris; it's about preparing the home for its new chapter, ensuring that every surface shines and every corner is pristine.

Cabinet and Countertop Finishing: Cabinets and countertops are more than just storage and work surfaces; they are central to the home's daily life. The installation of these items is done with precision, ensuring that doors align, drawers glide smoothly, and surfaces are sealed and polished.

Floor Finishing: The flooring receives its final treatment, whether it's sealing tile grout, applying the finishing coat to wood floors, or stretching carpet to perfection. The floor finishing process is vital for both the appearance and longevity of the flooring.

Appliance Testing: Once connected, appliances are tested to confirm their functionality. This includes running the dishwasher through a cycle, testing the microwave, and ensuring that all appliances are in perfect working order.

Final Inspection: A final inspection is conducted to ensure that every aspect of the interior finishes meets the quality standards set forth at the project's inception. This inspection covers everything from the smooth operation of cabinet doors to the proper sealing of countertops and the flawless finish of the floors.

Ready for Occupancy: With the final finishes complete, the home stands ready to welcome its occupants. The transition from construction site to living space is now complete, and the doors are open for the homeowner to begin making memories in their new home.

This chapter serves as a guide for builders and homeowners alike, emphasizing the importance of attention to detail and quality craftsmanship in the final stages of home construction. It is these final touches that turn a house into a home, ready for laughter, love, and life that will fill its rooms.

Considerations for Homeowner Turnover:

- The residence is on the brink of completion, awaiting the final handover to the homeowner.

- A final meeting is typically arranged between the builder's sales representative and the future homeowner to confirm that all finishes meet the agreed-upon standards and expectations.

Construction Activities for Final Finishes:

- **Cabinetry and Countertops**: These essential elements of the home's interior are installed, providing both functionality and aesthetic appeal.
- **Flooring Installation**: Following the completion of other interior finishes, the installation of the finish flooring commences. This includes laying down tile, wood, carpet, or linoleum in accordance with the design plan, adding warmth and character to the home.
- **Appliance Connection**: Key appliances, such as the dishwasher and microwave, are connected to their designated outlets, ensuring that the home's kitchen is fully operational.

- **Final Construction Clean**: A comprehensive cleaning is undertaken to prepare the home for its new inhabitants, ensuring that it is spotless and welcoming.

Finalizing interior finishes can be a complex process with several challenges:

1. **Material Durability**: Ensuring that the chosen materials are durable and suitable for their intended use is crucial. Materials must withstand daily wear and tear, especially in high-traffic areas.
2. **Aesthetic Consistency**: Achieving a consistent look that aligns with the homeowner's vision and the overall design scheme can be difficult, particularly when coordinating multiple finishes.
3. **Installation Quality**: Poor installation can lead to issues such as misaligned tiles, improperly hung cabinets, or visible seams in flooring.
4. **Maintenance Requirements**: Some finishes may require more maintenance than anticipated, leading to increased long-term costs and effort for the homeowner.
5. **Color Matching**: Ensuring that colors match between different batches of materials, such as paint or tiles, can be challenging.
6. **Cost Overruns**: Staying within budget while achieving the desired quality and style can be difficult, especially if unexpected issues arise during installation.
7. **Time Management**: Coordinating the completion of various finishing tasks within the project timeline can be challenging, especially if there are delays with material delivery or installation.
8. **Functionality vs. Design**: Balancing practical functionality with design aesthetics is a common challenge, as some design choices may not be the most practical for everyday use.

By anticipating these challenges and planning accordingly, builders and designers can mitigate potential issues and ensure a smooth finalization of interior finishes.

Innovative solutions to common interior finish challenges include:

1. **Advanced Laser Leveling Systems**: To address uneven surfaces, advanced laser leveling systems are used to ensure precision in installations.
2. **Moisture-Resistant Drywall Materials**: These materials help prevent issues like mold and structural damage due to moisture.
3. **Flexible Joint Compounds**: These compounds accommodate minor movements within walls, reducing the risk of cracks.
4. **Prefabricated Drywall Panels**: These panels can speed up installation times and improve quality control.
5. **Acoustic Drywall for Soundproofing**: Specialized drywall that enhances soundproofing capabilities for quieter interiors.
6. **Biophilic Materials**: Incorporating natural elements into interiors to create a more organic and inviting space.
7. **Smart Surfaces**: Utilizing materials that can change color or pattern based on environmental factors or user interaction.
8. **3D-Printed Elements**: Customizable and intricate designs made possible by 3D printing technology for unique finishes.
9. **Recycled and Sustainable Materials**: Using eco-friendly materials that reduce environmental impact and promote sustainability.
10. **Digitally Printed Finishes**: High-resolution digital printing on surfaces like tiles and wallpapers for custom designs.

These solutions not only address the challenges but also open up new possibilities for creativity and functionality in interior design.

Summary & Key Takeaways: Final Stages of Interior Finishes

Transition to Homeownership:

- The completion of interior finishes signifies the transformation of a construction site into a homeowner's sanctuary.
- A final walkthrough ensures every finish aligns with the homeowner's vision and the home's design specifications.

Cabinetry and Countertops:

- The installation of cabinets and countertops marks the embodiment of the home's functionality and style, reflecting the homeowner's taste.

Flooring Installation:

- The choice of flooring material—tile, wood, carpet, or linoleum—significantly impacts the home's ambiance, comfort, and acoustics.

Appliance Connection:

- Connecting essential appliances like dishwashers and microwaves is crucial for a fully operational kitchen from day one.

Final Construction Clean:

- A thorough clean-up prepares the home for its new chapter, ensuring a pristine environment for the new occupants.

Precision in Finishing:

- Precision in installing cabinets and countertops is key, with attention to aligned doors, smoothly gliding drawers, and polished surfaces.

Floor Finishing:

- The final treatment of floors, whether sealing, coating, or stretching, is vital for their appearance and longevity.

Appliance Testing:

- Testing appliances to confirm their functionality is essential, ensuring everything is in perfect working order.

Final Inspection:

- A comprehensive inspection guarantees that all interior finishes meet the quality standards established at the project's inception.

Ready for Occupancy:

- With the final finishes in place, the home is ready to welcome its occupants, marking the start of new memories.

This chapter highlights the importance of meticulous attention to detail and quality craftsmanship in the final touches that make a house a home.

Chapter Twelve: Maintenance

"Another flaw in the human character is that everybody wants to build and nobody wants to do maintenance."

Kurt Vonnegut

Home maintenance is an ongoing process that preserves the integrity, safety, and comfort of a residential house. This chapter delves into the essential practices of both ongoing and preventative maintenance that homeowners should adopt to safeguard their investment and enhance their living experience.

Understanding Home Maintenance: Maintenance tasks can be categorized into two types: ongoing and preventative. Ongoing maintenance includes regular tasks that keep a home functioning smoothly, such as cleaning gutters or servicing HVAC systems. Preventative maintenance involves actions taken to prevent future problems, like sealing cracks in the foundation or insulating pipes to prevent freezing.

Ongoing Maintenance Tasks:

- **HVAC Servicing**: Regularly replace filters and schedule annual inspections to ensure heating and cooling systems are operating efficiently.
- **Plumbing Checks**: Inspect for leaks, clogs, and wear in pipes and fixtures to avoid water damage and costly repairs.
- **Electrical System**: Test smoke detectors, GFCI outlets, and circuit breakers to ensure they are in good working order.
- **Roof and Gutters**: Clean gutters and downspouts to prevent water buildup and inspect the roof for damaged shingles or potential leaks.

Preventative Maintenance Strategies:

- **Foundation Care**: Check for cracks or signs of movement in the foundation and address them promptly to prevent structural issues.
- **Weatherproofing**: Seal windows and doors to prevent drafts and improve energy efficiency.
- **Pest Control**: Regularly inspect for signs of pests and employ measures to deter them from entering the home.
- **Landscaping**: Maintain trees and shrubbery to prevent overgrowth that could damage the home's exterior or foundation.

Seasonal Maintenance Tips:

- **Spring**: Focus on exterior maintenance such as painting, sealing decks, and starting up irrigation systems.

- **Summer**: Prioritize landscaping, pest control, and checking the integrity of outdoor living spaces.
- **Fall**: Prepare for colder weather by servicing the heating system, cleaning the chimney, and winterizing outdoor plumbing.
- **Winter**: Keep walkways clear of ice and snow and monitor the house for ice dams or excessive snow load on the roof.

The Role of Home Inspections: Regular home inspections can identify potential issues before they become major problems. It's advisable to have a professional inspection every few years, or when considering a renovation or sale.

Creating a Maintenance Schedule: A well-organized maintenance schedule helps homeowners stay on top of tasks. This can be a simple checklist or a detailed calendar of when to perform each task, taking into account the home's specific needs and the local climate.

The Importance of Maintenance Records: Keeping detailed records of maintenance activities, including dates, costs, and service providers, can be invaluable for tracking the home's condition and for resale purposes.

Effective home maintenance is about being proactive rather than reactive. By regularly performing both ongoing and preventative maintenance tasks, homeowners can ensure their house remains a safe, comfortable, and valuable asset for years to come. This chapter serves as a guide to establishing a robust maintenance routine that will help protect one of life's most significant investments.

Common mistakes in home maintenance can lead to costly repairs and decreased home value. Here are some key errors to avoid:

1. **Neglecting Regular Inspections**: Failing to regularly inspect key areas like the roof, HVAC system, and plumbing can lead to major issues going unnoticed.
2. **Ignoring Small Problems**: Small issues like a leaky faucet or a crack in the wall can escalate into bigger, more expensive problems if not addressed promptly.
3. **Improper Use of Appliances**: Overloading circuits or not cleaning appliances can reduce their lifespan and efficiency.
4. **Forgetting to Replace Filters**: Not changing HVAC filters regularly can lead to poor air quality and strain on the system.
5. **Skipping Seasonal Maintenance**: Each season requires specific maintenance tasks that, if skipped, can lead to damage and higher energy costs.
6. **DIY Without Skills**: Attempting repairs without the necessary skills can result in improper fixes and further damage.
7. **Not Following a Schedule**: Lack of a maintenance schedule can lead to overlooked tasks and inconsistent care.

8. **Overlooking Safety Precautions**: Safety steps like testing smoke detectors and securing heavy furniture are often forgotten but are crucial for home safety.

By being proactive and attentive to these common pitfalls, homeowners can maintain their property effectively and avoid unnecessary expenses.

Creating a personalized home maintenance schedule involves assessing your home's specific needs and organizing tasks based on their frequency. Here's a step-by-step guide to help you create an effective schedule:

1. **Assess Your Home's Needs**:
    - Conduct a walkthrough of your home and note areas that require regular maintenance.
    - Identify tasks that need daily, weekly, monthly, or seasonal attention.
2. **Set Realistic Goals**:
    - Consider your lifestyle and time constraints.
    - Ensure your schedule is manageable and aligns with your availability.
3. **Time Management**:
    - Allocate specific time slots for maintenance tasks in your weekly routine.
    - Decide whether to spread tasks throughout the week or tackle them in one go.
4. **Prioritize Tasks**:
    - Rank tasks by importance and frequency.
    - Focus on critical tasks that impact your home's functionality and safety.
5. **Use a Calendar**:
    - Add each task to a home maintenance calendar.
    - Consider using digital calendars for reminders and easy adjustments.
6. **Seasonal Adjustments**:
    - Plan for seasonal maintenance activities, such as servicing your HVAC system before summer or winter.
7. **Maintain Records**:
    - Keep a log of all maintenance activities, including dates, costs, and service details.
    - This will be helpful for tracking and future reference.

By following these steps, you can create a personalized home maintenance schedule that keeps your home in top condition while fitting into your lifestyle. Remember to review and adjust your schedule as needed to accommodate changes in your home or personal circumstances.

Here's a basic framework you can adapt:

Monthly Tasks:

- **HVAC Filters**: Check and replace them if necessary.

- **Water Softener**: Check salt levels and replenish if needed.
- **Drains**: Inspect and unclog sink and tub drains.
- **Safety Devices**: Test smoke alarms and carbon monoxide detectors.
- **Electrical**: Inspect cords for wear and test GFCI outlets.
- **Appliances**: Clean the dishwasher filter and run a cleaning cycle.

Seasonal Tasks:

- **Spring**:
    - Service HVAC system.
    - Clean gutters and downspouts.
    - Inspect roof and exterior for damage.
- **Summer**:
    - Check deck and patio for necessary repairs.
    - Maintain landscaping and garden.
    - Inspect and repair fences and gates.
- **Fall**:
    - Prepare your home for winter; insulate pipes.
    - Clean and inspect the fireplace and chimney.
    - Seal gaps in windows and doors.
- **Winter**:
    - Monitor for ice dams and icicles.
    - Check basement for leaks during thaws.
    - Inspect and tune-up major appliances.

Annual Tasks:

- **Roof**: Inspect for damage or leaks.
- **Foundation**: Check for cracks or signs of movement.
- **Exterior**: Paint and repair siding as needed.
- **Plumbing**: Have a professional inspection for leaks or corrosion.
- **Fireplace**: Clean and inspect if you use it regularly.

Record Keeping:

- Maintain a logbook or digital record of all maintenance activities, including dates, costs, and any warranties or service provider information.

Remember to adjust the schedule based on the age of your home, local climate, and specific circumstances. Regular inspections can help you catch issues early and adjust your maintenance plan accordingly.

Chapter Summary: Home Maintenance Essentials

Key Takeaways:

- **Maintenance Types**: Distinguish between **ongoing maintenance** (routine tasks for smooth operation) and **preventative maintenance** (actions to avoid future issues).
- **Ongoing Tasks**: Regularly service HVAC systems, check plumbing, test electrical systems, and clean gutters to maintain home functionality.
- **Preventative Strategies**: Address foundation issues, weatherproof homes, control pests, and manage landscaping to prevent damage.
- **Seasonal Tips**: Adapt maintenance activities to the season, focusing on exterior upkeep in spring, landscaping in summer, heating system prep in fall, and snow management in winter.
- **Home Inspections**: Schedule professional inspections to catch issues early, ideally every few years or before major changes.
- **Maintenance Schedule**: Create a personalized schedule to track tasks, considering the home's needs and local climate.
- **Record Keeping**: Maintain detailed records of maintenance for tracking and resale purposes.

By embracing a proactive approach to home maintenance, homeowners can preserve their home's integrity, safety, and comfort, ensuring it remains a cherished asset. This chapter provides a blueprint for a comprehensive maintenance routine that safeguards a home's value and the well-being of its occupants.

Chapter Thirteen: Safety

"An ounce of prevention is worth a pound of cure."

Benjamin Franklin

Construction safety is a critical aspect of residential building projects, ensuring the well-being of workers and the integrity of the construction process. This chapter discusses the essential safety measures and Occupational Safety and Health Administration (OSHA) standards that must be adhered to during the construction of residential houses.

Understanding OSHA Standards: OSHA provides comprehensive guidelines to minimize hazards in residential construction. These standards cover various aspects of construction safety, including fall protection, electrical safety, and the handling of materials and equipment.

Fall Protection: Falls are the leading cause of fatalities in construction. OSHA mandates the use of fall protection systems such as guardrails, safety nets, and personal fall arrest systems when workers are exposed to fall hazards.

Electrical Safety: Electrical hazards pose significant risks on construction sites. OSHA standards require proper grounding of electrical equipment, use of GFCI outlets, and regular inspections of electrical systems to prevent electrocution.

Material Handling: Proper handling and storage of construction materials are vital to prevent injuries. OSHA standards dictate safe practices for lifting, using powered industrial trucks, and storing materials to avoid accidents.

Hazard Communication: Workers must be informed about the potential hazards of chemicals and materials they are exposed to. OSHA's Hazard Communication Standard ensures that all hazardous materials are properly labeled and that safety data sheets are available.

Personal Protective Equipment (PPE): The use of PPE is essential to protect workers from various hazards. OSHA requires that appropriate PPE, such as hard hats, safety glasses, and gloves, be provided and used by workers at all times.

Training and Education: OSHA emphasizes the importance of training workers on safety practices, the use of equipment, and emergency procedures. Adequate training reduces the risk of accidents and injuries.

Creating a Safe Work Environment:

- **Safety Inspections**: Regular safety inspections of the site, equipment, and tools are necessary to identify and mitigate risks.

- **Emergency Preparedness**: Sites must have clear emergency response plans, including evacuation routes and first aid provisions.
- **Safety Culture**: Encouraging a culture of safety where workers feel empowered to report hazards and stop work if necessary is crucial for a safe construction environment.

Compliance and Enforcement: Adherence to OSHA standards is not only a legal requirement but also a moral imperative to protect workers. Non-compliance can result in penalties, legal action, and harm to the company's reputation.

Safety during the construction of residential houses is paramount. By following OSHA standards and implementing robust safety practices, construction sites can operate efficiently while safeguarding the health and safety of all workers. This chapter serves as a reminder of the importance of construction safety and the need for continuous commitment to upholding the highest safety standards.

For detailed information on OSHA standards and safety practices, it is recommended to consult the OSHA guidelines and participate in OSHA-approved training programs.

Ensuring construction safety on your residential project involves a comprehensive approach that includes understanding and implementing OSHA standards, using proper equipment, and fostering a culture of safety. Here's a summary of steps to take:

1. **Understand OSHA Standards**: Familiarize yourself with OSHA guidelines specific to residential construction, which cover fall protection, electrical safety, material handling, and more.
2. **Fall Protection**: Implement fall protection systems such as guardrails and safety nets, especially where fall hazards exist.
3. **Electrical Safety**: Ensure all electrical equipment is properly grounded and GFCI outlets are used to prevent electrocution.
4. **Material Handling**: Follow safe practices for lifting, moving, and storing construction materials to prevent injuries.
5. **Hazard Communication**: Keep workers informed about the potential hazards of chemicals and materials they might encounter.
6. **Personal Protective Equipment (PPE)**: Provide workers with the necessary PPE, including hard hats, safety glasses, and gloves, and ensure they are worn at all times.
7. **Training and Education**: Conduct regular training sessions on safety practices, the use of equipment, and emergency procedures.
8. **Safety Inspections**: Perform regular safety inspections of the site, equipment, and tools to identify and mitigate risks.
9. **Emergency Preparedness**: Have clear emergency response plans, including evacuation routes and first aid provisions.
10. **Safety Culture**: Encourage a culture where workers feel empowered to report hazards and stop work if necessary.

11. **Compliance and Enforcement**: Adhere to OSHA standards to avoid penalties and ensure the safety of all workers.

Remember, a safe construction site not only protects workers but also ensures the smooth progression of your project.

Summary & Key Takeaways: Construction Safety in Residential Projects

- **OSHA Standards**: Adherence to OSHA guidelines is essential for minimizing hazards in residential construction, covering fall protection, electrical safety, and material handling.
- **Fall Protection**: Implementing fall protection systems is crucial as falls are the leading cause of fatalities in construction.
- **Electrical Safety**: Regular inspections and proper grounding of electrical equipment are required to prevent electrocution risks.
- **Material Handling**: Safe practices must be followed for lifting, using equipment, and storing materials to prevent injuries.
- **Hazard Communication**: Workers should be informed about the hazards of materials they handle, with all hazardous materials properly labeled.
- **Personal Protective Equipment**: PPE like hard hats, safety glasses, and gloves must be provided and used by workers to protect against various hazards.
- **Training and Education**: Training workers on safety practices and emergency procedures is vital to reduce the risk of accidents and injuries.
- **Safe Work Environment**: Regular safety inspections, clear emergency response plans, and a culture of safety are key components of a safe construction site.
- **Compliance and Enforcement**: Compliance with OSHA standards is a legal and moral imperative to protect workers, with non-compliance leading to penalties and reputational damage.

Construction safety is paramount for the well-being of workers and the success of the project. Following OSHA standards and fostering a commitment to safety practices ensures efficient operation and the health and safety of all workers. For comprehensive safety guidelines, consulting OSHA's resources and training programs is recommended.

Chapter Fourteen: Technology

"Let's go invent tomorrow instead of worrying about what happened yesterday."

Steve Jobs

The construction industry is undergoing a technological revolution, with innovative tools and software reshaping the landscape of residential house building. This chapter delves into the cutting-edge technologies that are setting new standards for efficiency, accuracy, and safety in construction projects.

3D Capture and Modeling

3D capture technology has revolutionized the way architects and engineers visualize and plan residential structures. Tools like laser scanners and photogrammetry software create detailed three-dimensional models of construction sites, allowing for precise measurements and the ability to foresee potential issues before they arise. This technology not only streamlines the planning phase but also enhances communication among stakeholders by providing a tangible representation of the project.

Drones: The Eye in the Sky

Drones, or Unmanned Aerial Vehicles (UAVs), have become indispensable in modern construction. They offer a bird's-eye view of the construction site, enabling project managers to monitor progress, conduct inspections, and track equipment without setting foot on the ground. Drones can quickly survey large areas, produce topographic maps, and even assist in the transportation of lightweight materials.

Virtual Reality (VR): Immersive Planning

Virtual Reality has taken the concept of visualization a step further by immersing users in a fully digital environment. VR allows clients and builders to 'walk' through a virtual model of the home, experiencing the space as it would be in reality. This immersive experience is invaluable for making design decisions, identifying clashes, and gaining approvals without the need for physical prototypes.

Augmented Reality (AR): Enhanced On-Site Vision

Augmented Reality overlays digital information onto the real world, providing construction workers with valuable data directly in their field of view. AR can display plans, measurements, and simulations over the physical environment, reducing errors and enhancing the understanding of complex structures. It serves as a bridge between the digital plans and the physical construction process.

Mixed Reality (MR): Blending Worlds

Mixed Reality combines elements of both VR and AR, creating an environment where real-world and digital objects coexist and interact. MR enables architects and builders to overlay holographic models onto a physical space, offering a unique perspective on how the finished structure will integrate with its surroundings. This technology is particularly useful for renovations and extensions, where blending new with old is crucial.

Artificial Intelligence in Construction: A Transformative Approach

The integration of Artificial Intelligence (AI) in construction marks a revolutionary shift in the industry's approach to project management, design, and execution. AI's ability to mimic human cognitive functions such as problem-solving and pattern recognition has paved the way for smarter, more efficient construction processes[1]. Machine learning, a subset of AI, employs statistical techniques to enable systems to learn from data iteratively, enhancing their performance and predictive capabilities over time.

In the realm of construction, AI is instrumental in optimizing project lifecycles, encompassing design, bidding, financing, procurement, and even asset management. The utilization of AI-driven analytics and machine learning algorithms allows for the early identification of potential schedule risks, informed by a multitude of factors including historical data, weather patterns, and real-time project progress. This proactive approach to risk management can significantly reduce cost and schedule overruns, two of the industry's most persistent challenges.

Moreover, AI and machine learning are redefining safety protocols by analyzing job site data to predict and prevent accidents before they occur. Robotics, another AI application, is transforming construction sites with automated machinery that can perform repetitive tasks more accurately and tirelessly than human workers. This not only boosts productivity but also alleviates labor shortages by allowing human workers to focus on more complex and creative aspects of construction.

The adoption of AI in construction also extends to legal and regulatory compliance, where AI systems can navigate through complex codes and regulations to ensure adherence to legal standards. By automating the monitoring and reporting processes, AI facilitates a smoother compliance workflow, allowing construction professionals to concentrate on the physical aspects of building.

As AI continues to evolve, its potential to transform the construction industry grows exponentially. It offers a future where construction projects are safer, more efficient, and more aligned with the evolving demands of society. The embrace of AI in construction is not just about keeping pace with technological advancements; it's about reshaping the industry to be more resilient, innovative, and human-centric.

Construction Management Software: The Digital Backbone

Construction management software has become the digital backbone of the construction process, integrating various aspects of project management, from scheduling and budgeting to collaboration and documentation. There are multiple platforms that offer cloud-based solutions that streamline operations, improve communication, and ensure that all team members are aligned with the project goals.

The adoption of new and emerging technologies in residential construction is not just a trend but a necessary evolution. These tools are transforming the industry, making it possible to build smarter, faster, and safer homes. As we continue to embrace these innovations, the future of construction looks more promising than ever.

MacIntyre/Residential Construction: understanding the Basics.

Chapter Fifteen: Legal Matters

"If a builder build a house for someone, and does not construct it properly, and the house which he built fall in and kill its owner, then that builder shall be put to death."

The Code of Hammurabi

The construction of a residential house is not only a complex architectural and engineering feat but also a significant legal undertaking. This chapter delves into the legal requirements, contractual relationships, and potential litigation considerations that are integral to residential construction.

Legal Requirements for Construction Before breaking ground, it is imperative to understand and comply with local construction laws. These include obtaining the necessary permits, adhering to zoning laws, and ensuring compliance with building codes and ordinances. The homeowner or developer must secure lot approval, ensuring the parcel is an approved building site. Zoning laws dictate land use and building types permitted on the land, while ordinances and covenants may impose additional restrictions.

Construction Contracts A pivotal aspect of residential construction is the establishment of clear contracts. The American Institute of Architects (AIA) provides standardized contract documents widely recognized as the industry standard. These contracts define the relationships and terms between the parties involved in construction projects.

- **Owner and Architect Agreement**: This contract outlines the responsibilities and compensation of the architect, and it sets the foundation for the design phase of the project.
- **Owner and Contractor Agreement**: This agreement details the payment structure, whether it's a stipulated sum or cost-plus fee, and includes provisions for a guaranteed maximum price.
- **Subcontractor Agreements**: These contracts specify the terms between the general contractor and subcontractors, covering aspects like scope of work, payment, and timelines.

Contracts Between Parties The construction process involves various stakeholders, each bound by contractual agreements:

- **Owners and Developers**: Enter into agreements defining the scope, budget, and timeline of the project.
- **Developers and Architects**: Collaborate through contracts that outline design responsibilities and project specifications.
- **General Contractors**: Engage with owners, architects, and subcontractors through contracts that govern the construction phase.
- **Product Suppliers**: Are bound by supply agreements that ensure the provision of materials as per the project's requirements.

- **Legal Counsel**: Is often retained to navigate the complex legal landscape, draft contracts, and address any disputes that arise.

Construction Defect Litigation Construction defect litigation arises when there are issues with the constructed property that reduce its value, causes harm, or property damage. Defects can be patent (obvious) or latent (hidden), and they can stem from design flaws, poor workmanship, or the use of inferior materials. Common types of construction defect adverse effects include structural failures, water intrusion, electrical problems, and mold.

The litigation process is complex and typically involves expert testimony to investigate the defect, determine the cause, and recommend remedies. Damages may include repair costs, decline in property value, and sometimes punitive damages if the defendant's behavior is found to be reckless or intentional.

Understanding the legal intricacies of residential construction is crucial for a successful project. Clear contracts, compliance with laws, and preparedness for potential litigations are key to safeguarding the interests of all parties involved. By adhering to these guidelines, homeowners, developers, and construction professionals can navigate the legal landscape effectively, ensuring a smooth construction process and a quality finished home.

To protect yourself legally during the construction of your home, consider the following steps:

1. **Understand Your Rights**: Familiarize yourself with local construction laws and your rights as a property owner.
2. **Construction Contracts**: Use standardized contracts, such as those provided by the American Institute of Architects (AIA), which clearly define the scope of work, payment terms, and other critical details.
3. **Hire Licensed Contractors**: Ensure that all contractors and subcontractors are properly licensed and insured. This can protect you from liability in case of accidents and ensure quality workmanship.
4. **Insurance**: Obtain a comprehensive insurance policy that covers construction-related risks, including property damage and personal liability.
5. **Legal Counsel**: Engage a lawyer experienced in construction law to review contracts, handle disputes, and provide legal advice throughout the project.
6. **Document Everything**: Keep detailed records of all transactions, communications, and changes that occur during the construction process.
7. **Inspections**: Have regular inspections conducted by qualified professionals to ensure that construction adheres to codes and standards.
8. **Construction Defect Litigation**: Be aware of the legal recourse available if construction defects arise and understand the process of construction defect litigation.

If a dispute arises during construction, it's important to handle it carefully to minimize disruption and potential legal issues. Here are steps you can take:

1. **Review the Contract**: Check the dispute resolution clause in your construction contract, which may outline specific steps for handling disputes.
2. **Communicate**: Attempt to resolve the issue through direct communication with the other party. Clear and open dialogue can often resolve misunderstandings before they escalate.
3. **Document Everything**: Keep detailed records of all communications, agreements, and actions related to the dispute.
4. **Consult Legal Counsel**: If the dispute cannot be resolved through communication, consult with legal counsel experienced in construction law for advice.
5. **Consider Alternative Dispute Resolution (ADR)**: Methods like mediation or arbitration can be less costly and time-consuming than litigation and often lead to a mutually agreeable solution.
6. **Litigation**: As a last resort, you may need to pursue litigation. This involves taking the dispute to court, where a judge or jury will make a decision based on the evidence presented.

Remember, the goal is to resolve disputes efficiently and fairly to keep your construction project on track.

Glossary

- **Rebar**: A reinforcing bar used to strengthen concrete, measured in eighths of an inch.
- **WWM**: Welded wire mesh, similar to rebar, used for reinforcing concrete.
- **Post-Tension Slab**: A technique where concrete is pre-stressed to enhance strength and span capabilities.
- **Hold-Down**: Hardware providing resistance to uplift forces on walls.
- **Concealed Barrier**: Components like WRB and flashing that are hidden but essential for moisture management.
- **WRB**: Weather-resistant barrier that acts as a secondary defense against water intrusion.
- **Flashing**: Materials that ensure continuity with the WRB and facilitate water shedding.
- **Waterproofing**: The application of materials to prevent water penetration.
- **Underlayment**: A layer between the roof deck and shingles or tiles that serves as a secondary weather barrier.
- **Composition Shingle**: A common roofing material made of asphalt, felt, fiberglass, and granules.
- **Concrete Tile**: Roofing tiles made of concrete, available in various profiles and colors.
- **Weep Screed**: A component that allows for drainage at the base of stucco walls.
- **Z-Bar**: A flashing piece used at horizontal terminations, such as the top of a stucco wall.
- **Head Wall**: The junction where a sloped roof meets a vertical wall.
- **Confined Rake**: The edge detail where a roof plane transitions to a vertical surface.

Epilogue

As we reach the conclusion of this comprehensive guide on residential construction, we reflect on the journey that transforms a mere concept into a tangible structure—a place called home. From the initial sketches on paper to the final nail driven into wood, each phase of construction is a testament to human ingenuity and the relentless pursuit of shelter and comfort.

Conclusion

The construction of a residential house is a symphony of various components, systems, and sequences, all meticulously orchestrated to create a harmonious whole. It is a process influenced by the immutable forces of nature and the ever-evolving standards of safety and efficiency. The journey begins with a vision, translated into detailed plans during the planning and development phase, which sets the stage for the transformation of raw land into a prepared site, ready for the foundation of a new beginning.

As trenches are dug and utilities laid, the groundwork for modern living takes shape, followed by the rise of frames that outline the future. This guide has navigated through the complexities of construction, shedding light on the importance of each phase, from the durability required to withstand environmental challenges to the precision needed for quality control.

In the end, the creation of a home is more than the sum of its parts. It is a sanctuary, a space that not only provides shelter but also holds the potential for memories and experiences. This document serves as a reminder of the meticulous care and attention to detail that goes into building not just houses, but homes that will stand the test of time and become the backdrop for life's most cherished moments.

As we close this chapter, let us carry forward the knowledge and insights gained, applying them to ensure that every home built is a safe, durable, and efficient space for generations to come. The future of residential construction is bright, with new technologies and methodologies on the horizon, promising even greater possibilities in the art and science of building homes.

Acknowledgments

I extend my deepest gratitude to all those who contributed to the creation of this book. My heartfelt thanks go to the construction professionals, architects, engineers, and tradespeople whose expertise and insights have been invaluable. I am especially grateful to my family, and close friends who shared their personal construction experiences. A special mention must be made of the technological innovators whose tools and software have revolutionized the industry, making this book a timely resource. Lastly, I thank you, the reader, for embarking on this journey with me, as we explore the art and science of building homes.

About the Author

Nate MacIntyre – Construction Science Forensics, LLC Owner, Principal Consultant, Regional Director PNW & Hawaii. Technical responsibilities include building envelope assessment, rehabilitation, and restoration. Mr. MacIntyre is a licensed contractor in Oregon, Washington, Idaho, and Alaska. Specific areas of expertise include design review, building envelope condition assessments, building component field testing and analysis, forensic investigation of building envelope failures, trade coordination, and project management. Mr. MacIntyre has spoken to various trade associations on a range of topics, including the risks of "green" design and construction, building envelope design, and waterproofing failure analysis.

Mr. MacIntyre has been involved in the construction industry for over 25 years, focusing on building science and building envelope issues. He began his building science career as a test and balance engineering technician with Northwest Engineering Services. He then took the role of Director of Technical Services and owner of Superior Air Quality. At both firms, Nate was responsible for air quality testing, systems repair, and calibration. He later transitioned to Project Manager, for firms specializing in building science, waterproofing, and forensic investigation. In this role, Nate inspected, consulted, and reported on construction defects for residential and commercial buildings. Additionally, he provided on-site project management and quality control, and acted as a liaison/advisor for project building owners, architects, subcontractors, project engineers, and building officials. Specialties include: Building envelope failure evaluation/analysis, Building envelope condition assessment, Building envelope design, Construction defect evaluation, and Construction management.